If Olive Trees Could Talk

Dava Louise Colcord

New Harbor Press
RAPID CITY, SD

Colcord/New Harbor Press
1601 Mt. Rushmore Rd, Ste 3288
Rapid City, SD 57701
www.newharborpress.com

Ordering Information:
Quantity sales. Special discounts are available on quantity purchases by corporations, associations, and others. For details, contact the "Special Sales Department" at the address above.

If Olive Trees Could Talk/Dava Louise Colcord. —1st ed.
ISBN 978-1-63357-411-3

Cover photo taken in Southern Spain by the author.

Contents

Acknowledgments

I spent many hours talking to the Lord about this book. I found it difficult to write about the hard times. At one point, I told the Lord that I was willing to throw the whole manuscript in the garbage dumpster if that is what He wanted. Through prayer and the guidance of the Holy Spirit, I present my story. May your heart be blessed.

God sends special people into our lives. I have many, but there are two that I want to thank for making this book possible.

I am thankful for Cathy Young, who spent hours going over the manuscript with a fine-toothed comb. She sprinkled it with commas in the right places and made sure I was writing in the correct tense. She encouraged me to keep on, keeping on. Cathy is one of those special sisters in Christ who intentionally uses her gifts and talents to further His Kingdom.

I am thankful for Susie O'Berski, who continues to walk through life with me. She is a sounding board for me. I can count on Susie to always point me toward Jesus. She read parts of the manuscript and pointed me to Jesus. I deleted parts and rewrote parts. She read other parts and provided affirmation that I was on the right track. Thanks for caring, dear Susie.

Praises are lifted to my Heavenly Father who continuously reminds me that "I can do all things through Him who strengthens me."

Introduction

God is the first storyteller and He has been writing His story before creation and will continue throughout eternity. He knew me when I was in my mother's womb. He has a plan for me and knows every thought. He loves me and guides me along life's path.

I started telling my story in my recent book *Up the River on a Leaky Junk*. I shared how God moved me, along with my husband, David, out of the corporate world and into missions. I related the ups and downs and near drowning experiences I encountered on my first five mission assignments.

My next mission trips were primarily around the Mediterranean. I was fascinated with olive trees. Their gnarled trunks seemed to express their individual personalities. Some olive trees are hundreds of years old. I wonder what their story would be if they could talk. I wonder what they would say about the time Paul and Barnabas went to Cyprus on their first missionary journey. "So, being sent out by the Holy Spirit, they went down to Seleucia, and from there they sailed to Cyprus." (Acts 13:4) Barnabas means "son of encouragement" and was a Jew from Cyprus. I'll tell you later about my mission trip to Cyprus and the thrill of retracing Paul's steps. I also found Paul's influence in Greece, Turkey, and Italy as I travelled there.

The Mount of Olives was named for the olive trees that once covered the area. Those olive trees must have heard Jesus tell two of his disciples,

> "Go into the village in front of you, where on entering you will find a colt tied, on which no one has ever yet sat. Untie it and bring it here. If anyone asks you, 'Why are you untying it?' you shall say this: 'The Lord has need of it.'" (Luke 19:30–31)

> And as Jesus rode down the Mount of Olives "The whole multitude of His disciples began to rejoice and praise God with a loud voice for all the mighty works that they had seen, saying, 'Blessed is the King who comes in the name of the Lord! Peace in heaven and glory in the highest!'" (Luke 19:37–38)

The olive trees must have wept with those mourning. Luke writes, "As they led Him away, they seized one Simon of Cyrene, who was coming in from the country, and laid on him the cross, to carry it behind Jesus. And there followed Him a great multitude of the people and of women who were mourning and lamenting for Him."

When I was thirty, I heard the Good News of Jesus and received Him as my Savior. Because of Jesus I have a story to tell and because He lives, I can face tomorrow. I look back at past days, some good and some not so good, but in both the good and not so good, I see His hand. I hope that you, too, will see His hand on your life. You also have a story!

I dedicate this book to the love of my life, David, who went to be with the Lord on March 28, 2014. Here we are shown standing on the shore of the Mediterranean Sea after a short drive through the olive groves and vineyards on Cyprus. Olives and wine, two staples of the local diet, with a loaf of good crusty bread and some cheese make a great meal.

CHAPTER ONE

Time Out

After our second mission trip to Hong Kong, David and I called time out and wandered through nine European countries over an eleven-week period. I planned the trip while on mission in Hong Kong with the help of Lonely Planet travel books. Since we each could only handle one rolling suitcase and a small carryon, I tore interesting pages out of the travel books and threw the rest away. I had met a missionary years before who was putting together a directory of mission guesthouses. He said if I gave him some entries, he would send me a copy when completed. Several of these mission guesthouses would be our haven as we ventured from one country to another.

Our destination was Atlanta, Georgia, after spending several months in Hong Kong. Just before going to Hong Kong, David's mother died and left him a small inheritance. David sought wise counsel from our friend Michael. During the eleven-week trip, the investment made thirty-two percent paying for the entire trip.

David and I found a good price on the air flight from Hong Kong to Zurich, Switzerland. In fact, it was a round-trip fare that allowed a stopover in Athens, Greece. We had no plans to return to Hong Kong, but this was a better price than a one-way ticket. We thought, since it was a long trip from Hong Kong and we would have jet lag, we would fly into Zurich and get on a train to Vienna. We could rest, sleep, and hopefully recover from the flight during the train trip.

We arrived in Vienna after dark. It was snowing and cinders were spread on the icy streets. As we pulled our rolling luggage along, the wheels picked up cinders. The cinders made pulling difficult and very soon David's wheels came to a halt and the handle broke off his luggage. Now, he had to bend to pull his luggage along, so he laid his carryon on top. In a few moments, we looked back. The carryon was no longer with him. We back-tracked and it was still there in the middle of the path. Whew!

We checked into a small hotel and, as I closed the drapes, I saw a man looking up toward our window. I had visions of being stalked from the train station and fear surged in my head. I was not thinking clearly due to lack of sleep. The next day, we set out along Mariahilfer Strasse to buy some warm tights, gloves and hats, since we had just arrived from subtropical Hong Kong.

I loved the Christmas market in front of the Rathaus (Town Hall); the twinkling lights, music that transcends language barriers, wide-eyed children tugging on their parents to move them closer to the candy counter. After touring the Schönbrunn Palace, we took in the Christmas market in front of the palace and sampled cherry dumplings with custard sauce. Next, we went to Saint Stephen's Cathedral, built in the twelfth century, and up over three-hundred steps for a great view of Vienna.

A couple of days sightseeing in Vienna revived us enough to take the train to one of Ian Thomas' Torchbearers International Bible schools. Schloss Klaus is a fairy-tale castle built in the eleventh century. It had been in ruins but was rescued and restored to its original beauty in the 1960s. Our room was one-hundred steps up; it is tough to be a princess.

It was a short walk from the castle to the train station. We took a day trip to Salzburg where *Sound of Music* was filmed.

The Festungsbahn funicular runs every few minutes up to the Hohensalzburg Fortress. Construction of the fortress began in 1077 and it is one of the largest medieval castles in Europe. I was to learn that David always wanted to go to the top of every cathedral and castle we visited. Although when we got to Ludwig's castle, Neuschwanstein in Füssen, Germany, I convinced him to take the horse-drawn wagon up the road to the top of the hill.

David and I had recovered from jet lag and took the train back to Zurich. Pricey Zurich, where a snack totaled about $40 US. We had contacted another of the Torchbearers' schools, so we had a reasonably priced room waiting for us at Hinterholz just outside of Zurich. We were able to use this as our base. Taking advantage of the great Swiss train system, we visited Interlaken, Grindelwald, Zermatt, the Matterhorn, and Luzern.

One morning, we started off early on a trip through the Alps. As the snow got deeper the train switched to a narrow-gauge rail. The magnificent Alps with sunshine peeking out made me want to sing "His Majesty." Passing St. Moritz, over the Bernina Pass, we reached the little town of Poschiavo on the Italian border. I remember when we got off the train, quarter-size snowflakes were sticking to my jacket. We had lunch at a warm, cozy restaurant and then caught the train back to Zurich, counting this day among one of our treasures.

One of our granddaughters was working as an *au pair* (nanny) for a family in Geneva. The trains were convenient in this part of the world and served our sightseeing well. Her host family was so gracious and invited us to stay with them. Geneva is deep in Reformation history and a visit to the Reformation Wall was a must. It honored many individuals of the Protestant Reformation with statues.

Next came a day trip to Montreux and Chillon Castle, which has stood for over one thousand years. One of our friends from

Hong Kong had married a man from that part of Switzerland, and we spent the afternoon with them at their Swiss chalet.

Our airline ticket included a trip to Athens, so we headed for a warmer climate in Greece. We stayed in a small hotel near the Acropolis. The hotel suggested we try the little restaurant just a few doors away. We located it and walked down the steps to its cellar location. We neither spoke nor read Greek, and the people in the restaurant spoke no English. They motioned us to the kitchen where we were able to look over the different dishes and point to what we wanted. Everything was delicious and we went back several days to sample their fare.

We visited the Acropolis and climbed up Mars Hill overlooking the Agora where Paul used the monument to the Unknown God to proclaim the one true God and how one could be reconciled to Him.

> "So, Paul, standing in the midst of the Areopagus, said: 'Men of Athens, I perceive that in every way you are very religious. For as I passed along and observed the objects of your worship, I found also an altar with this inscription: To the unknown god. What therefore you worship as unknown, this I proclaim to you. The God who made the world and everything in it, being Lord of heaven and earth, does not live in temples made by man, nor is He served by human hands, as though He needed anything, since He Himself gives to all mankind life and breath and everything. And He made from one man every nation of mankind to live on all the face of the earth, having determined allotted periods and the boundaries of their dwelling place, that they should seek God, and perhaps feel their way toward Him and find Him. Yet He is actually not

far from each one of us, for 'In Him we live and move and have our being'; as even some of your own poets have said, 'For we are indeed His off-spring.'" (Acts 17:22–28)

This was one of those significant moments in life when you realize you are standing where the apostle Paul stood. It was sort of unsettling to see an ambulance parked at the bottom of the hill. The marble hill had become very slippery over the ages and many tourists fell and were taken to a hospital. We survived the descent.

We learned that we could take an eight-hour ferry to the ancient town of Monemvassia. Hidden away from the rest of the world, Monemvassia is a town seemingly unaffected by the passage of time. The town is located on a small island off the east coast of the Peloponnese. The town and fortress were founded in AD 583. There is a new town of Monemvassia with a causeway through a tunnel to the old town. We made a reservation at a little hotel outside of the new town of Monemvassia.

During the ferry trip, we noticed a man in a plaid suit walking by and smiling. We smiled back. We arrived at Monemvassia after dark. We disembarked and followed the crowd along the concrete pier and noticed the man in the plaid suit. Upon reaching the new city we hailed a taxi and asked the driver to take us to the little hotel. He said all taxis were in service outside Monemvassia and he could not take us.

We saw a group standing in the square and soon heard Christmas carols being sung. We were enjoying the singing and at the same time wondering where we were going to stay. The man in the plaid suit came along and stood next to us. We asked him about a room for rent in the town and he pointed to a sign in the window of a nearby tavern. It was written in Greek and he told us that it was for a "room for rent." He called the number and it was available. Our new friend walked us over to the room. He asked if we would like to have dinner with him out in the old town. After leaving our luggage in the room, we walked out the causeway and through the tunnel into old Monemvassia. It was a breathtaking sight as we emerged into a cobblestone village that looked like it must be a movie set. We were soon to learn that the ancient village has been inhabited through the centuries and there still are no motor vehicles allowed.

As we walked along the main cobblestone street, our friend escorted us into a tiny restaurant. We enjoyed tasting a variety of Greek dishes and getting to know our new friend. He told us that he was part of a family that performs on the flying trapeze. We kept thinking that he must be an angel that God sent to help us. When we walked back toward the tunnel, we stopped at a jewelry designer and David bought me a lovely ring for Christmas.

We were tired and ready to climb into bed when we got to our room. We settled in for what we hoped to be a long winter's nap. Soon we felt something biting us. We smacked at the bug in the dark, but there was a dozen more for each one we killed. Finally, we could not stand it and turned on the light. There was blood on our bodies where we killed the mosquitos. We discovered the source of the problem; a three-inch pipe coming in the wall was allowing a steady flow of those culprits. David took one of the towels and plugged the pipe. We whacked at the remaining ones we saw on the walls and their dead bodies made red splotches on the whitewashed walls. When we could not see any more flying around, we crawled back in bed exhausted.

The next morning, we walked around the village. We had hoped to go to Olympia, the ancient site that hosted the original Olympic Games, founded in the eighth century. As we walked, we noticed a sign "bus tickets." We entered the office and there was a man sitting at a desk. He was reading and looked up to greet us. As we approached closer, we could see that he was reading a Bible. We asked, "Are you reading the Bible?" A big smile came over his face and he replied, "Yes, I am a born-again Christian. Are you?"

He went on to explain that he had recently accepted Jesus as his Savior. We told him about our "bug" experience and our desire to travel around the Peloponnese. He happened to have a room for rent and whisked us over to see it. It was just what we needed. He had cars for rent and gave us the keys to one. We asked about advance payment and an agreement. He just laughed and said, "Pay me when you get finished with it."

We spent Christmas Day exploring the southern part of the Peloponnese. What an adventure! We were driving along a hilly road and came upon a shepherd guiding a bunch of sheep across the road in front of us. I was driving and David was directing me through tiny villages. All the road signs were in Greek, so we had to feel our way through villages and hope we were on the main road. At one point, David said turn left and left I went until I became lodged between a house and a wall. The only way out was to back up. An old lady came out of the house to direct me as I backed up.

The next day, we saw our new Christian friend and he was delighted to tell us that his pastor in Sparta wanted us to come for lunch. We had wanted to visit Sparta, a city that had existed since the 500s. We also wanted to see Mystra, built in the 1200s and the seat of the governor of the Byzantine territories. At one time it had a population of 20,000.

We were warmly welcomed by the pastor and his family. After enjoying a wonderful meal, they told us about their church that was reaching many for Jesus. They sent us on our way to see Mystra. Mystra hugged a very steep foothill and the best way to see it was to start at the top and walk down through the winding alleys. We decided that I would drop David and I would meet him at the bottom. He promised he would take videos of the most interesting sights including the frescoes in the Monastery Church dating around 1350. We learned that in 1989 the ruins, including the fortress, palace, churches, and monasteries, were named as a UNESCO World Heritage site. When David arrived at the bottom, he described the many medieval houses and palaces he saw and the wonderful frescoes.

We wanted to get back to Monemvassia before dark because we had some mountain switchbacks to maneuver along the way. The next morning it was time to say good-bye to our new friends and board the boat headed for Athens. It was a windy day, and there were white caps on the water. Shortly after we set sail, the captain announced that we had to head back to land and then taxied the rest of the way to Athens. I am not sure what was more dangerous, the rocky water or the journey in a taxi around hairpin curves with drop-offs to the sea. It was a relief to finally get to Athens and stand on solid ground.

I love Greece and Greek food! We were able to take several tours to ancient sites and even a day boat trip to the islands of Aegina, Poros, and Hydra. I love the white buildings and the deep blue sea. Often, when walking along the streets, people would come up and talk to me in Greek, thinking I was Greek. In those days I had jet-black hair and an olive complexion.

We flew back to Zurich and continued exploring Europe with visits in Spain to Barcelona, Madrid, Avila, Toledo, Seville, Carmona, Ronda, and Costa del Sol. At the time, we did not realize that someday we would be living in southern Spain. Nor did we know that our love for Greek food would continue as we spent a year on the isle of Cyprus.

We rented a car and drove along the southern coast of Portugal. The car gave us the ability to explore little fishing villages along the way. We stopped for an early dinner and the restaurant owner had a small hotel on site. We booked a room and when it was time to turn in, he said he would lock us in since we were the only guests that night. Tired we dropped off to sleep only to be awaked by an urgent alarm. We didn't know what the alarm was for, fire or something else. David decided to find out and opened the door. We were startled to see a man standing on a chair just outside our door trying to disconnect the alarm. The next day we drove further west to Cabo da Roca, the westernmost point of the European mainland.

Back to Barcelona we took the high-speed train to Paris with sleeping accommodations. It made the six-hour journey comfortable and we arrived refreshed. We stayed in a missionary apartment in a small town outside Paris. It was winter and we were the only ones in the three-bedroom apartment for $17 per night. It was fun to return each day from busy Paris to the small town and go by the bakery for our daily baguette. We spent several days going into Paris and taking in the sites, including the Louvre, Eiffel Tower, a boat trip on the Seine, and enjoying the sidewalk cafes. We ventured down to Tours and took a tour of the Loire Valley chateaus; Chenonceau, Chambord, and Azay le Rideau.

Our Eurorail Pass also included some boat trips so we decided to take an overnight boat from Cherbourg to Rosslare, Ireland. Once there, we continued via train to Dublin where we spent a few nights. David's son-in-law had a friend who worked at Trinity College in Dublin. We visited him and he took us to the eighteenth-century Old Library to see the Book of Kells. The Book of Kells is one of the greatest masterpieces in both Irish art and early Christian art. It is an elaborately decorated and illustrated Bible made from calfskin and painted by hand.

After a side trip to Galaway, enjoying the pubs in Dublin with their comfort food, warm fireplaces, and lively Irish music, we were getting tired. We decided to call time out and go to Ian Thomas' Torchbearers Bible School in Capernwray, England. A ferry took us across the Irish Sea to Great Britain and a train through Liverpool to Capernwray Castle. We spent a week at Capernwray, a nineteenth-century castle just south of England's famous Lake District. We sat in on Bible classes. It was a refreshing time, both physically and spiritually.

As our trip was coming to an end in a few weeks, I started thinking about my old boss who I had worked for in Atlanta and was now in Little Rock, Arkansas. Thoughts of him would not go away. I even dreamed about him. We finally called him from Capernwray Castle, and he asked what we were going to do when we returned to the US. We said, "We don't know. We are headed back to Atlanta." He had taken a new position just a couple of months before at a church in Little Rock. He encouraged us to come by Little Rock before returning to Atlanta. We were able to change our ticket to Little Rock via New York City.

Now, refreshed and having a new destination in the United States, we took the train to London, our last stop before returning to the US. We stayed at the Foreign Missions Club that was opened in December 1893. The mission was to provide a safe, comfortable, and welcoming place for missionaries and their families to stay. In those years, many missionaries with their steamer trunks packed were heading off to faraway lands. Exhausted missionaries returning to London were delighted to find a place to stay to restore their weary souls and bodies.

In 2008, the name was changed to The Highbury Centre and it is open to all Christians. Retaining its original mission, the guesthouse still serves large numbers of missionaries and Christian workers. It continues to offer an oasis of calm and tranquility to all those in need of rest at a reasonable rate.

By now I was needing a haircut and got one at Harrods department store. Harrods' motto is "All things, for all people, everywhere." The motto is fitting because, throughout the entire history of Harrods, the store has sold a wide assortment of goods. It started with tea and groceries, then linens, drapes, and wickers, only to move into pretty much anything, including exotic animals. In the seventies and eighties, the store was targeted for bombing attacks. Harrods was in the news in 1997 when Princess Diana and Dodi, the millionaire son of Harrods' owner, Mohamed Al-Fayed, were killed in an auto accident.

Not far from Harrods was a discount shop that sold china, and I had held off on purchasing anything larger than my hand during our weeks of travel. Now, it was my turn to get a set of Portmeirion china that we could easily carry home on the airplane. I still use it daily and treasure each plate and bowl that brings back so many memories.

We took a hop-on hop-off double-decker bus tour around London. Our favorite stop was the War Rooms which were located beneath the Treasury Building. They became fully operational in August 1939, just a week before Britain declared war on Germany. It was interesting to see how life carried on underground. Winston Churchill became Britain's prime minister in May 1940. Germany had that same morning invaded France, Belgium, the Netherlands, and Luxembourg. Churchill later said, "I felt as if I were walking with destiny, and that all my past life had been but a preparation for this hour and for this trial. I thought I knew a good deal about it all, I was sure I should not fail." He delivered his famous broadcasts from the War Rooms and was declared "the only man we have for this hour."

After spending a couple of hours in the War Rooms we surfaced to the street with armed guards. We learned that a double-decker bus had been attacked while we were below. Our hop-on hop-off tour was now off permanently for the day.

During our time in London, we attended a Sunday worship service at All Souls Church, which was consecrated in 1824. John Stott spent more than fifty years in ministry at All Souls. He authored dozens of books including *Basic Christianity*. We had an opportunity to take a side trip to Canterbury.

Each of the nine countries we visited provided many good memories, but they produced culture shock. This was before the euro, so each country had its own currency, laws, language, food, etc. By the time we felt comfortable, it was time to leave and enter another country. We did have fun! The time of our lives! But we were ready to go back to the United States.

CHAPTER TWO

Little Rock

We flew into Little Rock on March 1st on a one-way ticket believing that it was the Lord's leading. Our pastor friend picked us up at the airport and we spent a few days at his house. A Scripture that the Lord gave us before leaving England ended up being the same one that the Lord had given our pastor friend when he was making his decision about the ministry position in Little Rock. "Forget the former things; do not dwell on the past. See, I am doing a new thing! Now it springs up. Do you not perceive it? I am making a way in the desert and streams in the wasteland." (Isaiah 43:18–19)

Within one week, we both had jobs on staff at our friend's church, bought a car, and bought a house. A house, yes! We had put down roots after nine years of mission trips, moving in and out of the country. The way the house purchase happened amazed us. It began in New Jersey where we visited David's oldest son and family before taking off for Little Rock. We linked up with their realtor who put us in touch with one in Little Rock. When we arrived in Little Rock, she showed us a home that was one year old but had only been lived in for six months before the owner was transferred. The fireplace had never been used. Since it had been on the market for six months, we were able to purchase it for $100 over what it had sold for new a year before. From contract to closing was nineteen days. On God's fast track!

I went to work as the associate pastor's administrative assistant. I immediately became involved in missions and coordinated the church's first mission conference. As the months went on, there was more and more interest in missions. In fact, I coordinated a prayerwalking trip to a closed country. Prayerwalking had been a new concept to me until I went on my first mission trip in Toronto among Muslims, Hindus, and Sikhs. I read a book called *Prayer walking: Praying On-Site with Insight*. I learned that you pray as you walk where you expect God to answer prayer. Praying for the people who live there. Observing the surroundings and claiming the Lord's victory for them. At that time, I had no idea that years later I would lead a prayerwalking project in North Africa.

"Delight yourself in the Lord, and He will give you the desires of your heart." (Psalms 37:4) We had dreamed and talked about chartering a sailboat and sailing around the Virgin Islands. While in Little Rock, it seemed like it was a good time to fulfill that dream. We researched the many charter companies and sailboats available. One caught David's eye, the *Zulu Warrior*, a 1960 vintage with mahogany and teakwood interior. But it wasn't really the boat that excited David; it was the owner/captain. He was a graduate of Georgia Tech where David went to college. Dyke was seventy-five years old and Inge, his wife, was sixty-five. They had sailed those waters for over thirty years. This would be their last year of sailing and the boat was for sale.

We learned that Dyke received an aeronautical engineering degree from Georgia Tech. They ended up living on Long Island where he worked. One year they took a vacation to the Virgin Islands. They loved sailing and the Caribbean so much that they returned to Long Island, sold their house, quit his job, and moved to Saint Thomas. They bought a boat and began chartering.

We sailed with them out of Red Hook in Saint Thomas for a week. The best vacation we ever had. We didn't put on shoes all week and lived in our bathing suits. We showered by standing on deck, soaping up, and jumping overboard to rinse off. Inge would hose us off with fresh water when we climbed back on deck. We were so relaxed that most nights we would climb up into bed at 7:30 p.m. Inge was a great cook and we were provided three wonderful meals a day, plus a midmorning and afternoon snack. She was also Dyke's first mate and would haul up the anchor and hook the buoy when we went to anchor in one of their favorite spots. David loved to take the helm from time to time. They would ask us each day if we wanted to go ashore and shop and we would tell them we just wanted to sail.

A large boat named the *Atlanta* docked alongside us one day. It was a 110-foot beauty and Dyke said it was for sale for $17 million. It had a crew of seven and was owned by a prominent businessman from Atlanta. During the week the *Atlanta* seemed to be nearby most days or docked near us.

One day we sailed to a location near a cave at Norman Island. Inge fixed us a bag of bread. We snorkeled along the rock edge and at the entrance of the cave we let the bread float into the water. Fish came swarming, all sizes, all colors, such fun!

I celebrated my birthday on the boat as we sailed to Peter Island's Little Harbor. It was a very picturesque place with really calm, greenish blue water. The pelicans put on a show by diving for minnows. Inge made a special birthday dinner topped off by a luscious chocolate cake. We sailed to Marina Cay and put down anchor for the night. The next morning, Dyke took us to shore with the dinghy. We walked along the beach and to the top of the hill for the view. The gift shop was very expensive. We decided we were boat lovers and not land lovers and signaled for Dyke to come get us. We sailed to the Baths on Virgin

Gorda. Dyke took us ashore and we walked among the huge rocks. This is an amazing spot in the Caribbean and with a sailboat you can get closer than if you were on a cruise ship. When we were finished exploring, we swam back to the *Zulu Warrior*.

Another day we headed along the shore of Virgin Gorda. There was little to no wind, so we motored. Inga noticed the bilge was filling and Dyke cut the motor. The wind had picked up enough to sail and we sailed along the coast up to Necker Island. It was owned then by the president of Virgin Air and we were told that Princess Di had visited there once. We eventually sailed into the bay at Bitter End, a large British Virgin Island resort. Dyke had chosen this spot to repair the bilge. He dinghied us to shore where we took a swim in a freshwater pool and then enjoyed a warm shower. All for $3. Dyke had fixed the leaky hose and the alternator while we were on shore.

Some days we would just enjoy sitting on the bow watching pelicans fly through the sky with fluffy white clouds or dolphins jumping as we sailed along. What a lazy life! We enjoyed times with the Lord as we read and prayed surrounded by His marvelous creation. We had decisions to make about staying in Little Rock or what He wanted us to do.

When we returned to Little Rock, David and I pursued another mission assignment and this time with a very large denominational mission agency. The application process was intense, especially since we had both been divorced. We had to write a lengthy paper about our divorces and be interviewed by a counselor. We had to write about our beliefs, our salvation experience, biographies, submit references, have physicals, etc.

We had to meet physical requirements and we went on diets and lost about twenty-five pounds each. Walking three miles in the mall before we went to work was a daily routine. We had been waiting for the approval to come about our assignment in Cyprus. As we walked, we passed a display of the *Active Living* tabloid. I thought about picking up a copy on my next lap, which I did. Still keeping pace with David, I opened it some-where in the middle of the publication, directly into an article on Cyprus. My heart leapt! I knew it was the Lord confirming that we were going to Cyprus. Praise you, Jesus, for speaking. It doesn't matter when the approval officially comes, we have heard from you.

We continued by faith to market our house and, once again, from contract to closing was nineteen days. When the Lord wants you to move, He moves. We had to accept an offer $3,000 less than we had hoped for. That money was to be used toward purchasing computers for our mission assignment. The day be-fore the closing, we received a check in the mail from one of our prayer partners for $3,000. Amazing!

My son had just bought his first house in Texas and we loaned our furniture to him. Just a five-hour drive south. We needed to sell our car and advertised it for nine days and we had only two calls inquiring about it and no offers. After the evening service the night before we left Little Rock, a buyer surfaced. The next day we picked up the U-Haul and loaded our jumbo suitcases and a few antiques to take to our son in New Jersey. We drove to the bank, sold the car, and headed north. We had hoped to get $2,000 more from the car sale to put toward the comput-ers. Three weeks later, while at the missionary training center, we decided one evening to sell $2,000 worth of stock the next morning. Then, we got an email from one of our prayer part-ners. He said he suspected that the $2,000 he sent our church to be used for our computers might not have reached us. We replied it hadn't. Within twenty-four hours a $2,000 check was deposited in our checking account. We didn't need to sell stock. Praise Jehovah Jireh, the Lord provides.

My ongoing prayer for our team in Cyprus was to be of one accord, have unity. I had seen so much discord in the Little Rock church from the day I arrived. If we, as children of God, will spend eternity together praising the Lord, why can't we put down our selfish ambitions and envy and be unified in our praising of Him here on earth. I had been reading Revelation and read about the seven churches—all in Turkey. They had their problems, too. Perhaps we can visit these locations someday. Mighty churches are now ruins in a land filled with Muslims.

Revelation 7:9–10 describes a great praise service less traditional than most of us are accustomed to in our church. "After this I looked, and behold, a great multitude that no one could number, from every nation, from all tribes and peoples and languages, standing before the throne and before the Lamb, clothed in white robes, with palm branches in their hands, and crying out with a loud voice, 'Salvation belongs to our God who sits on the throne, and to the Lamb!'"

Unity in the midst of diversity! If the Cyprus team will focus on praising Him, we will have unity among our diversity. "May the God of endurance and encouragement grant you to live in such harmony with one another, in accord with Christ Jesus, that together you may with one voice glorify the God and Father of our Lord Jesus Christ. Therefore, welcome one another as Christ has welcomed you, for the glory of God." (Romans 15:5–7)

We made it over the mission agency hurdles and were accepted as Strategy Coordinators (SC) for an unreached people group located in a Middle Eastern country. We were to work with a Rapid Advance Team in an office in Cyprus among other SCs who were assigned one or more of the many people groups of our target country. Since I do not want to reveal the country and endanger anyone, I will refer to it as "Narnia." I read that more have become Christians in the last twenty years than in the previous thirteen centuries since Islam came to Narnia. In 1979, there were an estimated five hundred Christians from a Muslim background and today . . . some say more than one million. Christianity is the fastest growing religion today in that country.

We went through several weeks of training at the mission headquarters including training about our people group. While in training, we received a call from the Rapid Advance Leader (RAL) who told us that the assignment for our people group had been given to someone else quite some time ago and he had inadvertently not removed it from the personnel request form. He assured us not to worry, but when we got to Cyprus, we would receive another people group assignment.

CHAPTER THREE

Cyprus

C yprus is one of the largest islands in the Mediterranean. It had been under British control since the late 1800s, until in August 1960, Cyprus became a republic. Turks and Greeks lived on the island, but it was plagued with violence between the Greek and Turkish communities. In 1974, a Greek military coup, which aimed to unite the island with mainland Greece, led to a Turkish invasion and the division of the island between Turkish Northern Cyprus and the Greek Cypriot Republic of Cyprus. The island was divided, and Turkish Cypriots occupied the northern third of the island and the Greek Cypriots the southern part. Cyprus remains divided to this day and has the only divided capital left in the world, Nicosia.

The mission provided a place for us to live and use of a car. We were to live in a house with four bedrooms, so we could host others coming for temporary assignments. In the back of the house was living quarters for our landlady. Since we had been on several mission assignments, we had learned that if you want a comfortable bed you need to take your own. We shipped our mattress and two small recliners. So glad we did. When we left, we gifted them to missionaries.

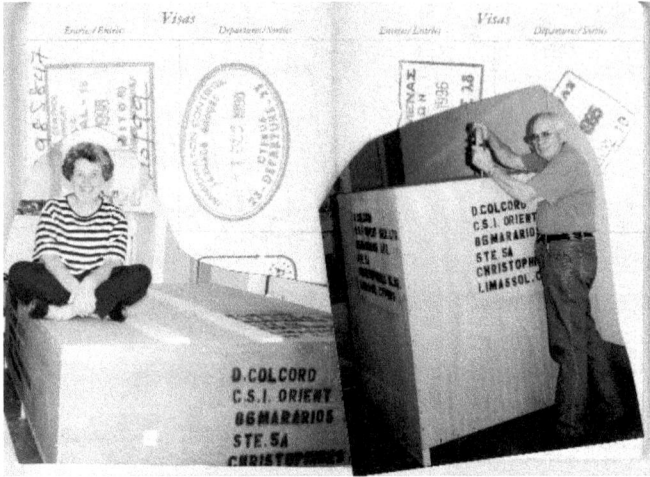

When we arrived in Cyprus the Rapid Advance Leader met us at the airport and David rode in the front seat with him. I was in the back with his wife and I overheard the RAL asking David if he thought I would mind being his Administrative Assistant. David and I talked later and felt that would fit my administrative and organizational gifts. David had the gift of service so he would assist in any way needed. We both were added to the Rapid Advance Leadership Team.

My desk was set up right next to the RAL's so I would be near to respond to any of his needs. During those first couple of weeks that I worked in the RAL's office, I heard from his leadership team and the Strategy Coordinators about a multitude of projects. As he came up with a new project/vision, I would write it down. More were added each day with no one apparently assigned or given direction for implementation. I also heard lots of mumbling, grumbling, and frustration from the Strategy Coordinators as well as other members of the leadership team about the RAL's lack of leadership. Lights began to go on—the RAL was a visionary and every morning he woke up with another vision or two or three.

My organizational skills were in motion. I began to write the name of each vision/project on a separate sheet of paper. I also made a list: (1) Who was assigned to this project?, (2) Definition of project, and (3) Project timeline and so forth. When I had a stack, I asked the RAL if he could help fill in the blanks. He said we should have a leadership team meeting and ask them. We did and we came out of the meeting with the majority of the projects abandoned since no one had the answers to the missing links. The result was that pressure declined and people were now able to focus on their assignments. Morale improved.

There was to be a missionary conference in Kuala Lumpur, Malaysia. Our whole team, including the children, totaled about one hundred and everyone was going. My job was to coordinate the round-trip flights for everyone for this 8,000-mile journey. Not only was our team attending, but other teams working in the Middle East were flying in for the meeting. I believe a whole hotel was taken over for this multiday event. A speaker was flown in from the United States to bring the Word of God and encouragement to all. I often wonder what the total expense was for that one conference and, if that money had been used to win people to Jesus, how many would be added to the Kingdom.

Back in Cyprus, I was asked to coordinate Henry Blackaby's visit. Henry Blackaby is known for his best-selling study course, *Experiencing God*. It was his first visit to Cyprus, and he would speak in several churches in Limassol where our team lived, in Larnaca, and Nicosia, the capital.

I enlisted team members to provide his local transportation and meals. He was a blessing and David and I had the privilege of showing Henry and his wife, Marilynn, some of the ancient sights. We spent the day with visits to Limassol Castle which was built around AD 1000 by the Byzantines. On to the archaeological ruins of Kourion which were destroyed in a severe earthquake in AD 365. We continued our sightseeing with a drive along the Mediterranean to the location of an amphitheater that

was believed to be built in the second century. It had been restored and was used for musical and theatrical performances.

Photo taken in front of our house in Cyprus.
Left to right, David, Dava, Henry, and Marilynn.

Nearby was a restaurant where we stopped to have lunch.
The menu was written on a blackboard and read, *"large fish dinner, small fish dinner and lasagna."* We ordered and Marilynn
said she was not very hungry and would have the small fish dinner. Marilynn was shocked when the waitress arrived with her
dinner of small fish fried with their heads on. We all learned
that we don't always interpret messages as the person providing
them intends. We had a fun day! We were sad to say goodbye
when the Blackabys left Cyprus.

One morning, we woke up to the strangest sky we had ever
seen. It looked like an eclipse, but we hadn't heard one was due.
When we went outside, we discovered everything was covered
with sand. What on earth had happened? We would soon learn
that we had experienced our first sandstorm, a *sirocco*, caused
by strong winds that pick up Saharan dust and carry it across
the Mediterranean.

Cyprus was a small country and we spent some weekends driving around exploring the ancient sites. In the town of Paphos, we saw the pillar Paul was said to have been tied to when he received thirty-nine lashes before converting his tormentor to the Lord. Paphos was full of ancient sites including an extensive complex of Roman buildings whose exquisite floor mosaics on ancient mythology were perhaps the best in the eastern Mediterranean. Other sites of Paphos included a lighthouse, the marketplace, a castle, the old customs house, the Roman theater for musical presentations, and the Turkish baths.

With access to the sea or mountains, every turn in the road brought a surprise. Driving in Cyprus was an adventure, since we had to drive on the left side and continue to remember that as we whizzed down the road. It took the two of us to drive. Our car had the steering wheel on the right with a standard shift on the driver's left. That was challenging. I would drive and put in the clutch and David would shift from the passenger seat. He would frequently shout, "Keep to the left." More adventure than I wanted. Of course, the natives could tell us Americans when they saw our windshield wipers go on instead of turning signals. The signals on the steering wheel were in different places than we were accustomed to. I am still messed up on left and right to this day.

One day we drove up to the foothills of the Troodos mountains to the village of Kakopetria. It had been inhabited since the seventh century and has about thirteen hundred residents. The old village was picturesque and designated as a historical site. We came upon the Old Mill Restaurant and stopped to have lunch. To our surprise, the young girl cleaning the tables was Chinese. After spending a year in Asia, we could speak a few words in Chinese. She was equally surprised. We discovered that she was from Mainland China. We promised to come back in a few weeks. We brought her a Chinese Bible. We never discovered how she ended up in this remote Cyprian village. Still a mystery, but maybe someday we will meet up in heaven.

I loved our drives through the little villages and back roads. One day, we started following one of the back roads and it turned to a dirt road. Then to a narrow road hugging a hillside and a drop off on the other side. Again, maybe a little too much adventure for me. We were committed and couldn't back up, so on we continued, discovering an abandoned village with only one family living there. It had been a Turkish village with a mosque and minaret. The abandonment was the result of the 1974 conflict when the Greeks had stayed in the south and the Turks fled to the north.

Living in another culture always brought new learning experiences and challenges. It looked strange to us that the cars parked up on the sidewalk and people had to walk in the road. City water was only available on certain days, so we had to schedule washing clothes on those days. There was a reservoir on the roof that filled so that there was some water on the off days. We could not flush the toilet paper. Instead, we placed the soiled tissue in a special little container that later was emptied into the trash for weekly pickup.

Our landlady invited us to attend her Greek Orthodox church one Sunday. David, who had a habit of crossing one leg on top of the other, was told quickly to put it down. We learned that to show the sole of your shoe to someone is like cursing. This was also a custom of Muslims.

We had the privilege of attending a Greek wedding and the groom was marrying for the second time. His two-year-old son cried during the early part of the service, so the groom left the altar and returned holding his little boy. A sweet gesture!

Easter Sunday we were invited to go to our landlady's parents' village. The food was so yummy. We learned more about growing olives and how the oil is pressed. Our landlady was always bringing us fresh pressed olive oil from her parents' trees.

I loved the olives we could get at the corner store. They had barrels filled with different kinds. I would take a plastic bag and scoop in as many as I wanted to buy. I think I became addicted to olives while I was in Cyprus and had withdrawals when I left.

Lazarus, who Jesus raised from the dead, was said to have come to Cyprus and became the first bishop. But we found another Lazarus that we frequented often. It was the name of a wonderful take-out restaurant where we could pick up moussaka, stuffed grape leaves filled with ground lamb or beef (sometimes both) and rice stuffing. We also had *pastitsio*, a baked pasta dish including ground beef and béchamel sauce, and for dessert baklava. And I always had olives in the refrigerator.

But for the best Greek meal, we would go for a meze where we were served a variety of small dishes followed with grilled meats. Then, strangely, they would bring a platter of French fries. We could call and let them know how many were coming and drive out of town and up a dirt road high up on a hill. A young couple owned it and it was our favorite place to go.

Living on Cyprus, we had easy and reasonable access to several other countries. Ferries ran out of Limassol to Israel but, every time we were going to spend a weekend in Israel, there were rockets going off. I am sad we missed that opportunity. But I was thrilled at being able to get a great price on a trip up the Nile that began with a short flight to Cairo. The all-inclusive trip included being met at the airport and transported to a lovely hotel, the Marriott Cairo, an old palace. The historic palace was originally built in 1869 to provide for guests during the Suez Canal inauguration celebrations.

The hotel was located on the Nile River where we took a walk to explore the area. We were surprised when we noticed guards with machine guns standing in the doorways of local businesses. It brought back memories of being in Manila, Philippines, where we witnessed the same thing. That evening, we were taken to the Sound and Light Show at the pyramids in

Giza. Cairo's traffic is an adventure where lanes are multiplied based on the urge of drivers. No one seemed to notice the lane markings, everyone was jockeying for position. A two-lane road can suddenly become filled with four cars next to each other. Horse-drawn carts, donkeys, and a bunch of sheep all walked down the road among the cars. As we approached the pyramids, we saw camels and horses. What a madhouse!

It was a cold evening and we rented a blanket as we sat and watched the laser show against the pyramids and the Sphinx constructed between 2589 and 2504 BC. I had never thought that I would visit the pyramids and still be within the city of Cairo. I had envisioned them to be located somewhere out in the desert.

The next day, we were driven to the airport to fly to Luxor to pick up our cruise. The area between Cairo and Luxor was noted for its terrorist activity. Just months before we visited this area, sixty-two Germans were killed at a major tourist attraction across the Nile River from Luxor. Tourism was at a new low and most of the boats were parked. There are normally 20,000 tourists per day in Luxor. Out of two hundred fifty boats, only seven were operating. As we flew from Cairo along the Nile, it looked like a wilderness; a desert for miles. The only thing green was near the Nile itself.

We boarded the one-year-old Nile cruiser. It had wood paneling inside and everything had an antique look. It normally holds one hundred ten people, but there were only nineteen of us for this cruise. One of the couples had been friends with one of Egypt's Ministry officials and he had provided them with a bodyguard. So, when we got off for our daily tour, we loaded on a bus with the bodyguard along. In front of the bus was a pickup truck with the back portion filled with men with machine guns. We were well-protected.

Valley of The King
Madina Habu
Luxor
Esna
Aswan
Karnak
Denderah
Edfu
Philae Temple
Komombo

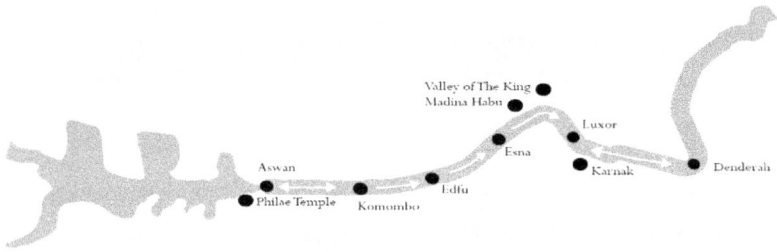

We sailed at night and each morning we woke up anchored in a new port. Ammon, our daily tour guide, had a degree in Egyptology. He made the ancient sites come alive. One day, when he was lecturing, he mentioned that he had done his thesis on the Pharaoh who chased Moses out of Egypt. Our ears perked up and we told him later that we would like to get together and talk about that subject further. We set a time to meet on the top of the boat.

We brought our Bible along and, as Ammon told his Pharaoh story, we turned to a Scripture that related. Ammon became very interested in the Bible and said he would like one. We asked if he would like it in Arabic and he said, "No, English, just like yours." He asked that we send the Bible to his home address in Cairo. Ammon told us he did his thesis based on historical accounts and the Koran.

At the time, one of my sons was working for Joshua's Christian Book Stores. We asked him to send the Bible to Randy at the mission headquarters. Randy had a trip planned to Cyprus and could bring it to us. Once we had the Bible, we learned another missionary was going to Cairo. The missionary called Ammon's wife and told her she had a gift from David and Dava. His wife exclaimed, "Oh, a Bible." The missionary was pregnant and when she delivered the Bible, she saw Ammon's wife was pregnant, too. They developed a friendship. Someday, we may learn the rest of the story. Hopefully, we will all meet in eternity.

Part of our team lived in Turkey and we were asked to visit them and provide some training. They lived in Istanbul that is in both Europe and Asia with the Bosphorus Strait separating the two. Because we lived in Cyprus on the Cypriot side and Cyprus is a country divided with the Turks, we were not allowed to fly directly to Turkey. We had to fly to Athens and then to Istanbul. We were met at the airport in Istanbul by our friends and taken by boat across the Bosphorus where we settled in at a small hotel. During the next days, we met with the team for training and they introduced us to Turkish cuisine. Really quite good. We especially liked the doner kebab and a dish made with eggplant.

They wanted to show us the old city of Istanbul on the European side. We went to the Grand Bazaar, one of the largest and oldest covered markets in the world. It is known as one of the first shopping malls. It initially started in 1461 after the Ottoman Empire's conquest of Istanbul. It covers sixty-one streets with over 4,000 shops. One could get lost in it. We kept our eye on our friends who were guiding us.

The Blue Mosque and Hagia Sophia were other locations that were a must. The Blue Mosque was built in the early 1600s and contains blue tiles in the interior. The exterior has six minarets. *Minaret* in Arabic means "beacon" and is used to call Muslims to prayer five times a day.

Hagia Sophia is a cathedral built in the sixth century under the direction of the Byzantine emperor, Justinian I. It remained the largest cathedral in all of Christendom in the Byzantine time, but became a Muslim mosque when Constantinople was conquered in 1453. It remained a mosque until it was converted into a museum in the 1930s. I read recently that, for the second time in its history, it has been turned into a mosque. In July 2020, a court annulled a 1934 presidential decree that made it a museum.

At the time we were in Istanbul, we found the city to be a city of contrasts. We saw women wearing burkas that completely covered them walking alongside women in tank tops. I haven't been back to the area to see what is happening, but I can cite a couple of things that make me think Turkey has changed. One is very personal. One of my granddaughters was living in Turkey and had to come back to the United States because of unrest in her location. Another is someone I prayed for. Andrew Brunson, an American citizen who lived in Turkey for twenty-three years, he was a pastor in a small evangelical Presbyterian church in the city of Izmir. He applied for a visa renewal in April 2016 and, six months later, was arrested and charged as a terrorist. He was held in prison for two years. Through prayer and the intervention God using the United States government he was released in October 2018. While in prison, he wrote a song and the chorus goes like this—

> You are worthy, worthy of my all
> You are worthy, worthy of my all
> What can I give to the Son of God,
> Who gave Himself for me?
> Here I am,
> You are worthy of my all.

During our stay in Istanbul, we had met another missionary whose desire, like ours, was to visit the actual sites of the Seven Churches of Revelation.[1] We made some phone calls and learned that the three of us could take a private tour of the ancient locations.

---

1. BibleStudy.org, "Map of Revelation's Seven Churches," https://www.biblestudy.org/maps/the-seven-churches-of-revelation-map.html.

The Seven Churches of Revelation

"I, John, your brother and partner in the tribulation and the kingdom and the patient endurance that are in Jesus, was on the island called Patmos on account of the word of God and the testimony of Jesus. I was in the Spirit on the Lord's day, and I heard behind me a loud voice like a trumpet saying, "Write what you see in a book and send it to the seven churches, to Ephesus and to Smyrna and to Pergamum and to Thyatira and to Sardis and to Philadelphia and to Laodicea." (Revelation 1:9–11)

We flew from Istanbul to Izmir, the city that was previously called *Smyrna*. We met up with our van and knowledgeable guide and spent three days exploring the history of the church sites. Bible in hand, we turned to the last book of the Bible, Revelation, chapters two and three. Our tour first took us to Ephesus that is located sixty miles south of Izmir.

"To the angel of the church in Ephesus write: 'The words of Him who holds the seven stars in His right hand, who walks among the seven golden lampstands. I know your works, your toil and your patient endurance, and how you cannot bear with those who are evil, but have tested those who call themselves apostles and are not, and found them to be false. I know you are enduring patiently and bearing up for My name's sake, and you have not grown weary. But I have this against you, that you have abandoned the love you had at first. Remember therefore from where you have fallen; repent and do the works you did at first. If not, I will come to you and remove your lampstand from its place, unless you repent. Yet this you have: you hate the works of the Nicolaitans, which I also hate. He who has an ear, let him hear what the Spirit says to the churches. To the one who conquers I will grant to eat of the tree of life, which is in the paradise of God.'" (Revelation 2:1–7)

Ephesus was where John lived before his exile and is the closest of the seven churches to the island of Patmos. It was thought that John penned Revelation while in exile on the island of Patmos. Ephesus was an ancient port city probably near the coast of the Aegean Sea. It was one of the most important commercial and religious cities in Asia Minor. Today, Ephesus is six miles inland, probably because of centuries of silting from the Cayster River.

Ephesus served as the "mother" church to the others, all of which were connected by the same Roman road. The temple of the goddess Artemis, Diana, ranked as one of the Seven Wonders of the Ancient World, was located there. Very little is left of the temple today. A few foundation stones and a column are all that marks the site that was larger than a soccer field. The Book of Acts tells us about a man named Demetrius who "was a silversmith who made silver shrines of Artemis brought no little business to the craftsmen." (Acts 19:24)

Their income from making silver idols was being threatened and they "gathered together, with the workmen in similar trades, and said, 'Men, you know that from this business we have our wealth.'" (Acts 19:25) Interesting! Could this be the same today? Could people feel challenged by the Word of God and fearful in losing their power or wealth?

> "And you see and hear that not only in Ephesus but in almost all of Asia this Paul has persuaded and turned away a great many people, saying that gods made with hands are not gods. And there is danger not only that this trade of ours may come into disrepute but also that the temple of the great goddess Artemis may be counted as nothing, and that she may even be deposed from her magnificence, she whom all Asia and the world worship. When they heard this, they were enraged and were crying out, 'Great is Artemis of the Ephesians!'" (Acts 19:26–28)

Our visit to Ephesus was memorable because we were walking on the same marble streets that Paul, John, and many other saints once travelled. As we stood in the third-century BC Great Theater, which once held 25,000 people and the acoustics were said to be perfect, we thought about Paul.

> "So, the city was filled with the confusion, and they rushed together into the theater, dragging with them Gaius and Aristarchus, Macedonians who were Paul's companions in travel. But when Paul wished to go in among the crowd, the disciples would not let him." (Acts 19:29–30)

Ephesus at that time was a cultural center with a population of about 300,000. The ruins of the two-story Library of Celsus, built in AD 135, is the famous facade depicting Ephesus. A humidity control system was used to protect the 12,000 scrolls of papyrus housed in the library. I read once that the cities were always trying to outdo each other for power, prestige, and influence. Ephesus, Pergamum, and Smyrna often competed to be the official center of the Roman imperial cult for the province. Pergamum had been famous for its library, so perhaps the Ephesians were trying to have the best center of learning.

Before leaving Ephesus, we visited a house where it was believed that the apostle John brought Mary, the mother of Jesus, to live in safety. We stopped by the Basilica of St. John, the site of the traditional tomb of John. We headed back to Izmir and stayed in a hotel for the night.

> "And to the angel of the church in Smyrna write: 'The words of the first and the last, who died and came to life. I know your tribulation and your poverty (but you are rich) and the slander of those who say that they are Jews and are not, but are a synagogue of Satan. Do not fear what you are about to suffer. Behold, the devil is about to throw some of you into prison, that you may be tested, and for ten days you will have tribulation. Be faithful unto death, and I will give you the crown of life. He who has an ear, let him hear what the Spirit says to the churches. The one who conquers will not be hurt by the second death.'" (Revelation 2:8–11)

The church faced strong Jewish opposition. There were many Jews in the city and even today several synagogues are located throughout the modern city.

Old Smyrna was believed to be founded around the eleventh century. Smyrna rose to prominence as a Greek city with its prime port location on the Aegean coast. Smyrna was known for its schools of science and medicine. In Paul's day, it was believed the city had a population of 100,000.

Smyrna, yes, you were rich. The name *Smyrna* means "myrrh," which was a crucial ingredient used to embalm bodies. It had the ability to retard the putrefaction of dead flesh. This type of embalming was used in Egypt and Judea. You may recall myrrh was one of the three expensive gifts the Magi brought after the birth of Jesus.

Smyrna has little excavated. Except for the agora, a theater that could seat up to 20,000, and sections of the Roman aqueduct, little remains of the ancient city. As we explored the ruins, we found a group of Iraqi Kurdish ladies selling their wares. We learned that there were about 6,000 Kurdish refugees living in the area.

We headed north about seventy miles and inland about fifteen miles to Pergamum. It is the northern most of the seven churches. Pergamum was founded in the eighth century BC and during Paul's time had a population of 150,000. Now, the modern city is called Bergama.

> "And to the angel of the church in Pergamum write: 'The words of Him who has the sharp two-edged sword. I know where you dwell, where Satan's throne is. Yet you hold fast My name, and you did not deny My faith even in the days of Antipas My faithful witness, who was killed among you, where Satan dwells. But I have a few things against you: you have some there who hold the teaching of Balaam, who taught Balak to put a stumbling block before the sons of Israel, so that they might eat food sacrificed to idols and practice sexual immorality. So, also you have some who hold the teaching of the Nicolaitans. Therefore repent. If not, I will come to you

soon and war against them with the sword of My mouth. He who has an ear, let him hear what the Spirit says to the churches. To the one who conquers I will give some of the hidden manna, and I will give him a white stone, with a new name written on the stone that no one knows except the one who receives it.'" (Revelation 2:12–17)

As we climbed the hill to some of the ruins, I commented on all the trees surrounding the hill. I was told that these were brought to the area and are the source of Bergama's famous pine nuts. Gold mining in Bergama is environmentally controversial since the cyanide that is used may have killed off olive trees.

The Scripture noted the "teaching of Balaam." When we descended the hill, we stopped at the ruins of an Egyptian temple where Balaam was worshipped. Pergamum's Christian community was said to be too tolerant of evil. In American culture today, Christians now face a choice to blend into society or stand out in this culture of compromise.

We visited an alabaster manufacturing location. Alabaster, we were told, comes in several colors, including brown and yellow tones. The color is determined by the depth it is in the ground. White alabaster is the most valuable and is almost gone now. This made me think of the Scripture above about "a white stone."

At this point in my writing, I took a break to take my daily walk outside. I live in a sixteen-story building for people ages sixty-two and older. The elevator stopped but was full. During this time of COVID-19, we are limited to two at a time on the elevator. As the door was closing, I heard one of the ladies say, "I went to a hypnotist and he put nice thoughts into my mind." Is this what God wants us to do? Go to a hypnotist? No, the Bible says, "Set your minds on things that are above, not on things that are on earth." (Colossians 3:2) "Finally, brothers, whatever is true, whatever is honorable, whatever is just, whatever is pure, whatever is lovely, whatever is commendable, if there is any excellence, if there is anything worthy of praise, think about these things." (Philippians 4:8) Thank you, Jesus, for a real live example. May we heed the warning to the church at Pergamum.

> "And to the angel of the church in Thyatira write: 'The words of the Son of God, who has eyes like a flame of fire, and whose feet are like burnished bronze. I know your works, your love and faith and service and patient endurance, and that your latter works exceed the first. But I have this against you, that you tolerate that woman Jezebel, who calls herself a prophetess and is teaching and seducing my servants to practice sexual immorality and to eat food sacrificed to idols. I gave her time to repent, but she refuses to repent of her sexual immorality. Behold, I will throw her onto a sickbed, and those who commit adultery with her I will throw into great tribulation, unless they repent of her works, and I will strike her children dead. And all the churches will know that I am He who searches mind and heart, and I will give to each of you according to your works. But to the rest of you in Thyatira, who do not hold this teaching, who have not learned what some call the deep things of Satan, to you I say, I do not lay on you any other burden. Only hold fast what you have until I come. The one who conquers and who keeps My works until the end, to him I will give authority over the nations, and he will rule them with a rod of iron, as when earthen pots are broken in pieces, even as I myself have received authority from My Father.

And I will give him the morning star. He who has an ear, let him hear what the Spirit says to the churches.'" (Revelation 2:18–28)

Very little excavation had been done in the area other than a Roman street, part of a public building, and several inscriptions and coins. It appears that gods such as Zeus, Artemis, Apollo, and Athena were worshiped in the city. Inscriptions found at Thyatira reveal the city had many trades, including wool, linen, leather, bronze, pottery, and dyes. One of the major industries was the dying of textiles.

During Paul's second missionary journey (Acts 16:13–15), the apostle Paul traveled to Philippi and met a woman named Lydia, a seller of purple, from Thyatira. After listening to Paul preach, she became so convicted that she, along with her entire household, were baptized. Lydia may have traveled back to Thyatira and spread the gospel.

> "And to the angel of the church in Sardis write: 'The words of Him who has the seven spirits of God and the seven stars. I know your works. You have the reputation of being alive, but you are dead. Wake up, and strengthen what remains and is about to die, for I have not found your works complete in the sight of My God. Remember, then, what you received and heard. Keep it, and repent. If you will not wake up, I will come like a thief, and you will not know at what hour I will come against you. Yet you have still a few names in Sardis, people who have not soiled their garments, and they will walk with Me in white, for they are worthy. The one who conquers will be clothed thus in white garments, and I will never blot his name out of the book

of life. I will confess his name before my Father and before His angels. He who has an ear, let him hear what the Spirit says to the churches.'" (Revelation 3:1–6)

We travelled south to Sardis which had become an important Christian center during the fourth century. Sardis was the birthplace of coinage. Metallurgists discovered how to separate gold and silver producing both with surprising purity. Previously, the purity had been suspect, and hindered trade. Now, Sardis could mint nearly pure silver and gold coins that could be trusted throughout the known world. This economic revolution made Sardis rich.

In AD 17, Sardis was destroyed by an earthquake, but it was rebuilt with the help of 10 million *sesterces* (Roman coin) from the Emperor and exempted from paying taxes for five years. We saw the Roman Bath–Gymnasium complex with its Marble Court. We saw a section of the Royal Road. Our guide told us that the Royal Road was built from Sardis to Susa, now in Iran. He said mounted couriers were supposed to travel the 1,677 miles from Susa to Sardis in nine days. Previously, it would be a journey on foot of about ninety days.

> "And to the angel of the church in Philadelphia write: 'The words of the Holy one, the True one, who has the key of David, who opens, and no one will shut, who shuts, and no one opens. I know your works. Behold, I have set before you an open door, which no one is able to shut. I know that you have but little power, and yet you have kept My word and have not denied My name. Behold, I will make those of the synagogue of Satan who say that they are Jews and are not, but lie—behold, I will make them come and bow

down before your feet, and they will learn that I have loved you. Because you have kept My word about patient endurance, I will keep you from the hour of trial that is coming on the whole world, to try those who dwell on the earth. I am coming soon. Hold fast what you have, so that no one may seize your crown. The one who conquers, I will make him a pillar in the temple of My God. Never shall he go out of it, and I will write on him the name of My God, and the name of the city of My God, the new Jerusalem, which comes down from My God out of heaven, and My own new name. He who has an ear, let him hear what the Spirit says to the churches.'" (Revelation 3:7–13)

"I know that you have but little power, and yet you have kept My word and have not denied My name." Our guide felt this was written to those who struggle with weakness in their faith. Jesus' words of comfort certainly would have been a blessing to the Philadelphians who had faithfully stood for Christ in their pagan culture. His words continue to serve as an encouragement to faithful believers today.

We stayed the night in the Richmond Hotel in Pamukkale, a town in western Turkey that is known for its thermal waters. After dinner, we took a swim in the outdoor thermal pool, a first for me. The warm water relaxed my muscles and it was a refreshing experience.

The next day, we headed for Hierapolis which was founded around 190 BC with a well-preserved theater and a necropolis with sarcophagi that stretch for two kilometers. *Necropolis* means "cemetery," a large burial site. Hierapolis was not a very big settlement, but people came to this area for healing and the thermal baths. Many of them died and were buried here. Hierapolis and nearby Laodicea are mentioned in Colossians 4:13.

> "And to the angel of the church in Laodicea write: 'The words of the Amen, the faithful and true witness, the beginning of God's creation. I know your works: you are neither cold nor hot. Would that you were either cold or hot! So, because you are lukewarm, and neither hot nor cold, I will spit you out of My mouth. For you say, I am rich, I have prospered, and I need nothing, not realizing that you are wretched, pitiable, poor, blind, and naked. I counsel you to buy from Me gold refined by fire, so that you may be rich, and white garments so that you may clothe yourself and the shame of your nakedness may not be seen, and salve to anoint your eyes, so that you may see. Those whom I love, I reprove and discipline, so be zealous and repent. Behold, I stand at the door and knock. If anyone hears My voice and opens the door, I will come in to him and eat with him, and he with Me. The one who conquers, I will grant him to sit with Me on My throne, as I also conquered and sat down with My Father on His throne. He who has an ear, let him hear what the Spirit says to the churches.'"
> (Revelation 3:14–22)

When we visited Laodicea there was very little excavation. Laodicea grew due to the advantageous position on a trade route to become a very important city. There was extensive trade in black wool. It was noted for its banking centers. Eye salve was produced to treat medical conditions of the eye. The one major weakness was that they did not have an adequate water supply. Water had to be pumped from Colossae, which was eleven miles away, or Hierapolis, which was six miles away. By the time it arrived there via the aqueduct, the water was lukewarm. Lukewarm water, lukewarm faith? I pray that I will not become lukewarm but will finish this temporary journey on earth well.

This tour of the seven churches will live in my memory. I pray that I will seek first the kingdom of God and His righteousness. I pray that I will "bear fruit in old age" and "be green and full of sap" as written in the Psalms.

I remember Cyprus where we attended an International Church. One Sunday, I realized that ten young men from Narnia, our target country, were sitting behind me. Ten young men who had come to know Jesus as their Savior. Oh, that all of us believers would grasp the treasure we have in these earthen vessels and the power that the Holy Spirit has given us. We could turn the world upside down and win multitudes to Jesus.

Back in Cyprus, as the months passed, there was less and less for me to do. I had been able to do a lot of organizing and putting systems in place. I was essentially working myself out of a job. I looked for ways to help and talked frequently with the RAL about the idle time I had. There were days when he would come in and say, "Maybe we should send you over to live in Beirut," or other such places, depending on his morning vision. After a year, we said that we thought we were a waste of time and money for the mission and should return to the US. He finally agreed and we went home. Well, not home, because we had come to Cyprus from Little Rock, Arkansas. We had sold our home in Little Rock where I had worked for the Associate Pastor at a church there. I had worked for him in Atlanta, Georgia, several times between mission trips and, when I ended up in Little Rock working for him, I told him the next time he should move to a warmer climate. While I was in Cyprus, he took a job at a church in Naples, Florida. So, we were headed to Naples to work for him again.

CHAPTER FOUR

Naples

It was December and the *snowbirds* (that's what we called northerners who came south for the winter) flock to Southwest Florida at that time of year. Our pastor friend warned us that housing was scarce and pricey. Well, what to do now? I happened to talk about the problem with a missionary friend from another mission agency who was in Cyprus. She said, "My friend who stood up for me at my wedding lives there. I will email her." It wasn't long before she got back to me and said her friend had a guesthouse on her property where we could come stay until we bought our house." Praise the Lord! We ended up in Old Naples in the guesthouse of a delightful family.

Before leaving Cyprus, we had started looking for a condo over the Internet in the Naples area. We selected a realtor and got prequalified for a mortgage. During the weeks prior to leaving Cyprus, the Feds dropped the interest rates three times. That news drove the stock prices to increase. The market hit a new high. We were reaping the benefits of a strong market before we would need to sell in order to buy a house in Florida. I was over 59½ years old and could cash in my IRA without a penalty.

We arrived in Naples on December 2 and bought a condo, closed, and moved in on December 23rd. Wow! The Lord works fast. The condo was a newly built one in Pelican Landing in Bonita Springs. The day we looked at it, we loved it and made our offer. We learned that someone else had put an offer in just before us. I said, "If this is the place the Lord has for us, their offer won't stand." The other party had gone out to lunch and when they got back, we heard that they decided to wait for another building to be built and we got the condo we wanted. Praising the Lord and remembering His Word, "And He made from one man every nation of mankind to live on all the face of the earth, having determined allotted periods and the boundaries of their dwelling place." (Acts 17:26)

We moved into the condo. Well, David, I, and our luggage moved in. Our furniture was in Dallas where we had loaned it to one of my sons. After Christmas, we flew to Texas, loaded a truck, and drove back to Florida.

We started working for my pastor friend at his church in Naples. Even though we were back in the United States we were experiencing culture shock. I remember one day in a supermarket standing in front of the various brands of cereal. I was experiencing reverse culture shock. I had just come from places where more than one brand to choose from was unusual. We also missed periods in our own American culture. One of my sons mentioned something about being "politically correct." I questioned its meaning and then thought of the cultural change it reflected. Was this a new way devised to curtail discussion of certain topics?

I worked at the church as an Administrative Assistant to the Assistant Pastor of Administration. David and I were always involved in the mission ministry no matter where we lived. This church did not have a dedicated Missions Office and had never had a mission conference. We were able to coordinate their first conference and opened a Missions Office as Directors of World Missions.

I will never forget that first day in the Missions Office. I got a call from a man who said he would like to give his condo to the church to use for furloughing missionaries. I listened as he explained that he had been fortunate by making a lot of money and he wanted to give back. What a generous gift!

That same day, I received a call from a church member who said that he and his wife felt the Lord was calling them to missions. They came in and talked about their desire and the last I heard they were still on the mission field. Our desire to start a mission outreach was obviously the work of the Lord!

I love seeing the Lord work in lives time after time. I love to encourage men and women to take another step of faith in their walk with Jesus. Sometimes, it only takes a word or two inspired by the Holy Spirit to speak into a life. Other times, it may be something as simple as giving someone a copy of a book that was meaningful in your own life. You never know what the Lord is doing and going to do in someone's life. You might see the results, or you might never see the results. I gave a book one day to a young man, and the Lord revealed the results fourteen years later. You can read about it in the Life after David chapter.

During these months in the mission office, we were in contact with many missionaries. One missionary had been communicating her host country's needs in her prayer letters. As we prayed for her and her country, the question came to our mind: "What if we led a team from this church over there?" We began talking with our pastor friend about such an endeavor. It progressed from an idea to a reality.

The country name I will not reveal but I will tell you that it was not a place where Christians could openly share the Gospel. As we communicated with the missionary on the field, we realized that we could best help by putting together a business symposium. She talked with a university there and they were open to hosting a group of American businessmen and women. David and I put together a training program for the team members. We had spent time in countries closed to the Gospel and knew what we could say and what was best left unspoken.

We drew on our experience from directing the Friends from Abroad (FFA) outreach at the First Baptist Church of Atlanta. It was an outreach to international students from area colleges like Georgia Tech, Georgia State, Emory, Morehouse, etc. Most were graduate students completing their masters and doctorates. A good percentage of those who attended FFA were from Mainland China.

In order to enter our host's country, we had to have a visa. During the training process, there was one man who kept asking me what if we don't get the visa? What is our plan B? I tried to explain that faith works on God approving plan A, and if He doesn't, then you ask Him for a plan B. You don't need to have a plan B until God tells you to. So often we run ahead of God and do not wait on Him. I told him a story about what happened to David and I that taught us about waiting on God.

We took our youngest son back to college in Macon. I had the trip planned, taking a pillow along to sleep on the way back. It was about 9:30 p.m. and we were ready to head north to Atlanta on I-75. David suggested I drive, and that was fine since my son had given me an audio tape for the trip.

The car's clutch had been acting up and the music must have hidden the sound of it slipping. Before long, the car went slower and slower. As I saw trucks come speeding up behind me in the rearview mirror, I pulled off onto the shoulder. The car wouldn't pick up speed; now it wouldn't go over 40 mph. David said he would drive. He found that the clutch was getting worse and each hill was more difficult to climb. We had passed the town of Forsyth a few miles back. It was after 10:00 p.m., we were out among pine trees and the moon, and we were sitting on the shoulder of I-75. David took the pillowcase and started waving at trucks whizzing by as their breeze rocked the car. Finally, one pulled off the road a distance up front. The truck sat there. It seemed like a long time. Then we saw a man walking toward us. We had mixed emotions as we recalled the murder on I-75 the week before. David got out and walked up to meet the trucker and asked him to radio the State Patrol for help. No cell phones back in those days. The trucker was not too reassuring as he said, "I'll try."

When David got back in the car, I mentioned that Paul and Silas sang when they found themselves in jail. "Let's sing and maybe God will send an angel." Problem was neither of us could come up with a song. We finally managed two verses of "Jesus Loves Me." David kept trying to recall a praise song, humming, "Praise Him, Praise Him." What was the rest of that song?

An hour passed and no one stopped to help. David continued to wave at trucks and cars; in fact, he waved at everything that passed by. Another half hour passed, and suddenly I remembered the song. I sang out, "Praise Him, Praise Him, Jesus, My Blessed Redeemer." At that very moment, a pickup truck pulled in front of our car. David got out and walked up to the pickup. He asked the two men if they would give us a ride to the Route 16 exit where we could call some friends.

The men were dressed in suits and it appeared a safe move, safer than sitting on the side of I-75 at that time of night. We piled into the truck cab and I sat on David's lap. A book fell on the floor as the driver pulled back onto the highway. David thought he saw a Bible fall off the dash and he asked, "What do you fellows do?" "We're preachers and we just finished a revival down at Reidsville Prison." I exclaimed, "You are our angels."

David and I had been reading *Waiting on God* by Andrew Murray. This was indeed a lesson on waiting on God. God showed us His timing is perfect. We must wait and give God time to work both ends. Those preachers had to have time to finish the revival, get in their truck, and drive up I-75 to the point where God had chosen to do some of His rescue work.

"But they that wait upon the Lord shall renew their strength; they shall mount up with the wings as eagles; they shall run and not be weary; and they shall walk and not faint." (Isaiah 40:31)

Well, back to the trip overseas to do a business symposium. The visas came, the team was trained, and off we went. We flew first to Vienna and took our chartered bus to Schloss Klaus. In 1963, it was leased to Torchbearers, an international Bible school founded by Major W. Ian Thomas, an evangelical teacher often identified with the Keswick Convention ministry. We had the pleasure of hearing him personally in a church in Griffin, Georgia, years before. One year while living in Rome, Italy, we spent the Christmas holidays at another Torchbearers Bible School, Capernwray Hall. It is the same castle we spent a week at on our way home from Hong Kong. Torchbearers has twenty-five centers throughout the world dedicated to teaching and preaching the saving, indwelling, and transforming life of Christ.

Our training completed, we flew to our target country where we were met by our missionary friend. She had chartered a bus that took us to our hotel.

David and Dava at the back of the bus

We cautioned the team that our hotel rooms might be bugged. Welcome dinner and meeting new friends! The team presented business techniques at the university. Four of us went to a separate location to meet with Christians who had come from Muslim areas. David and I were thrilled to be part of helping Christians develop business plans. The Christian brothers and sisters related how they were discriminated against in a Muslim area and it was difficult to get jobs. These talented men and women each had a desire to start their own business. When the week came to an end, they each left with a plan that could be presented to other believers to raise support for their new endeavors. We shall not know the end of this story until we get to heaven.

Once our assignment was complete, we boarded the bus and were taken to an old communist headquarters that was now a spa. We enjoyed a massage for $5 before heading to the airport for our flight back to Austria. We returned to Schloss Klaus for our debriefing before heading back to Naples, Florida.

Plan A completed—no need for plan B.

CHAPTER FIVE

North Africa and Beyond

A mission-minded friend came to visit and brought a
video on "Prayerwalking in North Africa." The video
perked my interest, since I had coordinated a prayerwalking trip while in Little Rock. The video had been produced
by the same very large mission organization that David and I
had worked with in Cyprus. We learned that they were looking for someone to direct the project, to enlist and train prayer
teams, and to coordinate their trips to North African countries
like Libya, Tunisia, Algeria, and Morocco. The project would
not leave our minds as we prayed about it.

I remembered Simon of Cyrene who carried Jesus' cross to
the place of His death. (Matthew 27:32, Mark 15:21) Cyrene is
in modern-day Libya. And, at the day of Pentecost, there were
"Parthians and Medes and Elamites and residents of Mesopo-
tamia, Judea and Cappadocia, Pontus and Asia, Phrygia and
Pamphylia, Egypt and the parts of Libya belonging to Cyrene,
and visitors from Rome, both Jews and proselytes, Cretans and
Arabians . . ." (Acts 2:9–10) So, there was a thriving church in
North Africa. There were even missionaries that went to Antioch from Cyrene. "But there were some of them, men of Cyprus and Cyrene, who on coming to Antioch spoke to the Hel-
lenists also, preaching the Lord Jesus. And the hand of the Lord

was with them, and a great number who believed turned to the Lord." (Acts 11:20–21) There were martyrs like Perpetua and Felicity who were martyred in Carthage, now a suburb of Tunis, Tunisia. What happened to the church in North Africa?

Years later, I got a glimpse that helped to answer that question. While living in Southwest Florida I met a young lady from North Africa. I asked her questions about her family. She told me the name of the people group. I looked it up on the Joshua Project website that lists the many people groups in the world. They show general statistics of the people, their country, the various religions, and the number of known Christians. I learned that her father was from an unreached people group with no known Christian. The Joshua Project website described that people group and said, "Early generations kept their Christian heritage in secret and outwardly submitted to Islamic rule. The symbolism of the cross can still be found throughout their architecture, designs on handmade carpets, and even tattoos on women's faces. Today, however, they have no understanding of their Christian heritage." My new friend was raised Muslim and told me an interesting story about her grandmother. When her grandmother would drop an item, she would make the sign of the cross with her finger. This substantiated the information on the website. I read about the time Islam swept through North Africa in the seventh century. "They resisted Islam's advance ten different times in history outwardly saying they would become Muslims, but then returning to their villages and refusing to practice the religion. They intentionally built conspicuous white mosques at the top of the mountains to deceive Muslim invaders. As they passed, seeing the mosque in the distance, they would assume the village had already converted and continue on their way." Interesting!

During the time I was writing this, my friend from North Africa accepted Jesus as her Savior and I had the privilege of attending her baptism. Now, there is a known Christian in this people group. Praise the Lord!

David and I contacted the Regional Director and inquired about the assignment. To make a long story short, we were asked to fly to Nashville where we would meet the North African Field Director, John, and a Mississippi pastor who was involved in the project. We did and all agreed we should come on board as the Director of Prayerwalking for North Africa.

This was a project with a name and a video but no plan or policy in place. Our next step was to go to Mississippi for a week and write a procedure manual which was reviewed in detail and approved by the Mississippi pastor, the Regional Director, and the Field Director. We were to later learn that not everyone had bought into this vision, including the missionaries within country. This was the Field Director's vision, and not everyone would stand by their agreement.

We left for southern Spain where we would base the project. There were missionaries in that location but were not part of John's team. One had been enlisted to pick us up at the airport in Gibraltar and take us to the house that had been rented for us. The house had several bedrooms and was large enough to house teams who would come from the Unites States to do prayerwalking across the Gibraltar Straits in North Africa.

We arrived with several seventy-pound suitcases since we were to be there for two years. Jade and Sheila, a couple on another mission project, came along with the one enlisted to pick us up at the airport. Once they dropped us and the luggage at our house, they left. We had been given no orientation and no direction. We were left to fend for ourselves. We wondered what we had gotten ourselves into.

Getting over jet lag and unpacking faced us. I found a one-page map of the town, Algeciras, a port city in southern Spain on the Bay of Gibraltar. We ventured out one day to find the bus stop and hopefully locate the building where we would start the visa process to stay in Spain. We walked along the streets and asked a lady where the bus stop was. When the bus came, we asked if it was going to the city center and one of the passengers said it was. We did not speak any Spanish except "hello," "goodbye," and "thank you." It always amazes me how the Lord leads despite language barriers or other human limitations.

We found the immigration office and filled out the paperwork to begin the visa process. Jade and Shelah reached out to us and invited us over to their apartment for dinner. They told us that they were part of a two-year Journeyman Program with the same mission agency. Their mission was to a refugee group in North Africa. Shelah had grown up in Africa where her parents were missionaries. They told us that a good place to shop for familiar food items was a British supermarket in Gibraltar. During our stay in southern Spain they were so helpful. One day, we were able to help them when Shelah was very sick with malaria. We had a car and was able to take her to the doctor several miles away. She had contracted malaria originally when she was young and living in Africa.

A few years later, after they graduated from seminary, we heard that they became involved with former boy soldiers in Africa. *Boy soldiers* are children under the age of eighteen who are taken from their homes by armed groups and must serve in their armies. Most of the time, their homes have been destroyed and their parents killed. I read that there are an estimated 250,000 child soldiers in the world today in at least twenty countries. About 40% of child soldiers are girls, who are often used as sex slaves and taken as "wives" by male fighters.

We have kept in contact with Jade and Shelah and the following is from their website, *Refuge and Hope*.[2] It began as a small nonprofit supporting seven former child soldiers and two young street boys from southern Sudan. Jade and Shelah

---

2. Jade and Shelah Acker, *Refuge and Hope*, https://www.refugeandhope.org/about.

Acker who founded Refuge and Hope, started working with the boys while serving in a camp for former child soldiers in Sudan in 2001. Eventually, the camp was closed, and the boys were sent home.

In 2003, as the Ackers were preparing to return to the US, they learned that the rebel army that initially conscripted the boys into their ranks had intentions of recruiting them yet again. With the help of various friends and aid agencies, the Ackers devised a plan to get all nine boys to Kenya, where they would be safe from war and the possibility of being reconscripted into the military. The plan was a success, and that success was nothing short of a miracle.

Once the boys made it to Kenya, the Ackers enrolled them in boarding school and then headed back to the US to raise money to cover the boys' tuition and living expenses. While in the States, the Ackers spoke to friends, family members, and several church organizations about their situation. People responded by opening their hearts and their wallets. In 2004, the Ackers registered Refuge and Hope International as a 501c3 (nonprofit) organization to enable donors to make tax-free contributions and to ensure organizational accountability.

As more funds came in, Jade and Shelah saw an opportunity to serve refugees on a broader scale in Africa. Uganda—acting as a relatively stable home to more than 440,000 refugees from Congo, Sudan, Somalia, Eritrea, and other countries—seemed the logical place for relocation. Upon arriving in its capital city of Kampala in 2008, the Ackers worked to bring the boys from Kenya to Uganda while simultaneously launching an English as a Second Language (ESL) program and a Christian Discipleship program for a growing number of urban refugees.

Refuge and Hope's school, the Center of Hope, began with twelve students meeting in a small room in a heavily refugee-populated region in Kampala. Today, the organization serves more than 1,000 refugees a year and has expanded its programs to include educational, professional, personal, and spiritual development programs.

As for the nine boys the Ackers brought out of southern Sudan in 2003, they are now grown men building lives and families of their own. Jade and Shelah have two biological daughters and officially adopted the two youngest boys of the original group of nine—Angelo and Lino—into their family in 2013. In 2016, they officially adopted Meron, a refugee minor from Eritrea, into their family as well.

Both Angelo and Lino completed high school in Uganda. Lino and Angelo are currently in the US, living and working. Meron is currently in university. The girls are currently attending Acacia International School in Kampala. You can see the latest happenings on their website *https://www.refugeandhope. org/*. We are so thankful for Jade and Shelah's encouragement.

Our first prayerwalking team arrived from the United States. After a couple of days of briefing and training, we crossed the Gibraltar Strait to Tangier, a city in northern Morocco. It is only seventeen miles from the southern tip of Spain and is easily accessed by ferries that run regularly. Many Africans travel by ferry across the strait to work in Europe.

There are several missionaries located in Algeciras who distribute Christian literature including the *Jesus Film* at the port as Africans return to their homes. We became friends with several who had been doing this outreach for years.

Jade had made many trips across to Tangier and gave us some *dirham*, the legal tender in Morocco. He told us that when we got off the ferry, there would be taxis waiting to take us to the train station. He told us how many dirhams we should pay for the trip and to haggle with the taxi driver for that amount. He was right; it happened as he predicted.

We, along with the prayerwalking team, travelled to Fez, Marrakesh, and Casablanca by train. One of my impressions as

I looked through the train window was the many poor-looking shacks with a TV dish on top.

Fez was a fascinating city in northeastern Morocco. The old part was a walled medina with no automobile access. We saw donkeys pulling carts and the *souk* (an Arab market) was buzzing with people. We learned that the medina is the home to Islamic religious schools including one founded in the fourteenth century. It was elaborately decorated with cedar carvings and ornate tile work. We had the feeling that one could easily get lost in the medina, just like we felt in the Grand Bazaar in Istanbul. Our team prayer walked through the medina asking the Lord to open the hearts of the people.

Before leaving the medina, we visited one of the three tanneries located there. Tanneries have been a major part of Fez's economy since the city was founded in 789. We climbed to the third floor of a building to look down on the stone vats filled with hides. The odor was overpowering. We were told that they use a mixture of cow urine, pigeon feces, quicklime, salt, and water to clean and soften the skins. Men were in the pots working the skins with their feet. After this initial process, the hides are dyed with the use of natural colorants using poppy for red, indigo for blue, and henna for orange. Then, they are dried in the sun before going to craftsmen who produce the final product. This leather process uses only manual labor and the method has not changed since medieval times. Even today Moroccan leather is considered a very fine product.

Prayerwalking took us to Marrakesh, one of the most colorful cities I have ever visited. It is known as the Rose City because of the salmon-pink buildings that are built with natural red clay that comes from a nearby region. We had some American friends living there who showed us around. We ended the day at the ancient medina with its amazing souks. Outside the medina is the Jemaa el-Fna square and it was filled with many evening food stalls. Our friends had their favorite. The stall had a cooking area with a counter and benches surrounding it on three sides. Our friends greeted the cook in Arabic and ordered for us. The food was very good. Our friends told us that one of the dishes was spleen and then we were all suspect about everything we ate.

The next day we boarded the train for Casablanca. We were greeted by another American friend and had dinner at their home. We prayer walked through the huge Hassan II Mosque. The Hassan II Mosque is the largest functioning mosque in Africa and is the seventh largest in the world. Its minaret is the world's second tallest minaret, extending sixty stories topped by a laser that is directed towards Mecca. It was built in 1993 of handcrafted marble and has a retractable roof. A maximum of 105,000 worshippers can gather for prayer, 25,000 inside the mosque hall and another 80,000 on the mosque's outside ground. It cost over $700,000 to build in a low- to mid-income country. As we walked through the mosque, we asked the Lord to reveal the truth to the people who entered and the Spirit to draw them to Jesus.

We headed back to Tangier and, when we reached the port in Spain, we said goodbye to the team. A couple of weeks later, our American friends from Morocco came for a retreat about fifty miles down the road from us. We attended one of their meetings and afterwards began our drive back to Algeciras. We were driving along the divided highway with two lanes on each side. We were in the right lane and suddenly a car driving the wrong way in the other lane flew by us. That could have been a disastrous head on collision. We praise the Lord for His safety.

Within a few weeks, another prayerwalking team from the United States arrived. We met them in Madrid. We had coordinated their visit with a missionary couple living in Madrid. The team was housed in a nearby hotel, and the next day we met for orientation. This team later flew to Tunis, Tunisia, where they were met by another American friend. They prayer walked in several locations plus experienced a night in the desert.

I can't help wondering if the young lady from North Africa, who I met in Southwest Florida, was an answer to prayer as a result of the prayerwalking years before.

I have found that so often when you are involved in missions or ministry that some difficult trial comes your way. The Lord is interested in conforming us to His image. We were about to experience one of those difficult times, in fact, a series of difficult times. Looking back, we can praise the Lord for them, but in the midst, we were somewhat devastated.

A few weeks after the Tunisia team returned to the United States, we got a call from the Assistant to the Regional Manager. The same Regional Manager who had asked us to go to Nashville, the same one who asked us to go to Mississippi and put together a procedure manual that was approved by the Mississippi pastor, the same one who had sent us to Algeciras as Director of Praying Walking for North Africa. His assistant explained that the Regional Manager had discovered that there were two Directors for the project. The other one was the Mississippi pastor, so we were no longer needed. The mission would provide airfare back to the United States or we might inquire about another assignment with the mission. No further explanation was given. We only could speculate that one of the men who had been on the Morocco prayerwalking and had the ear of the Regional Manager and the Mississippi pastor had been involved in this decision.

We were in southern Spain, had leased our condo in Florida, and told we no longer have a mission assignment. What now? We felt like Jehoshaphat in 2 Chronicles 20:9, "If disaster comes upon us, the sword, judgment, or pestilence, or famine, we will stand before this house and before you—for your name is in this house—and cry out to you in our affliction, and you will hear and save." Verse 12 goes on to say, "O our God, will you not execute judgment on them? For we are powerless against this great horde that is coming against us. We do not know what to do, but our eyes are on you." Verse 15, "For the battle is not yours but God's." And finally, Jehoshaphat in verse 21 says, "And when he had taken counsel with the people, he appointed those who were to sing to the Lord and praise Him in holy attire, as they went before the army, and say, 'Give thanks to the Lord, for His steadfast love endures forever.'" Once again, we learn that the answer is to praise. Praise is an antidote for depression. Even when you don't feel like it, praise the Lord. It lifts your thought to the One who can do something about the situation and off yourself.

When we recovered from the shock, we began to think about the Rapid Advance Leader we worked with on Cyprus. We heard he had moved on to another project in Western Europe. We contacted him and he invited us to join his team. He was the project leader. He told us to come to Paris where he and the team were stationed.

We packed the seventy-pound suitcases once again. We would leave almost everything in Spain until we were settled in Paris. The day came when we were to fly to Paris and, early that morning, we got an email from the project leader. He asked us to call him. He explained that there had been some changes. The team was not going to live in Paris, but in Germany. He told us to fly to Paris and rent a car to drive to Germany. We had been selected to find the housing in Germany for the team members.

In Paris we met the team. In fact, we knew the assistant leader because he had been the assistant leader on Cyprus. His parents were also on the leadership team. So, after a few days, we rented a car and headed for Dachau, Germany.

We arrived in Dachau where we knew no one. But we knew the Lord who we depended upon to direct us. David, who is an excellent map reader and navigator, finally said, "I haven't the slightest idea where we are." He suggested I pull over and he would ask the waitress at a sidewalk cafe. We stopped at a cafe in the square and thought we would have lunch and get directions. The waitress spoke English and her brother, Marcus, just happened to be sitting at a table nearby with a friend and invited us to sit down. We learned where we were on the map and Marcus showed us how to read the want ads in a German paper in order to sort out apartments for rent. He was a law student in Munich and might be a good resource for translation in the future. We told him we were looking for a hotel and he suggested one just outside Dachau.

We were soon to learn that everyone knows everybody in this area. Ann Marie, owner of the hotel, told us to try her brother's place if we wanted a good restaurant. It was just down the road in a little village. She continued to tell us that it had been her parents' farmhouse and her brother had made it into a restaurant. She gave us directions and we had dinner there that evening. The food was wonderful, and they had rental quarters that were available. Now, our project leader and his family had a place to live while they looked for a more permanent home.

A real estate agent was searching for a place for us and we ended up renting a second-floor apartment in the nearby town of Odelzhausen. In Europe, when one rents an apartment, the kitchen comes with four walls and you are required to finish it. Also, you must install all the lighting fixtures. IKEA was a great resource for the items we needed. They help you lay out the kitchen and sell you the cabinets, appliances, and all the trimmings.

A trip to IKEA is quite an adventure. After completing the details for the items needed, we ate in the cafeteria. We sat down at a table with room for six and, when we returned from the food line, a lady and her two daughters were sitting at our table. We greeted them and then we said grace. When we looked up, the woman said, "Do you believe in Jesus?" When we answered yes, she stated they were born-again Christians. They invited us to their church which was located just a few miles from where we lived.

On Sunday, we drove through lovely little villages surrounded by beautiful green fields to get to the church. The area where the church was located had only three houses. It was the first free church in Bavaria. *Free church* means it is not associated with the government. This little church came into being when the King of Bavaria in the 1800s invited some Mennonites from another area to come and live in his country. He knew that Mennonites were good farmers and people that could be trusted. He built this little church.

We arrived late so everyone was inside. The church itself was a lovely soft pastel color nestled among tall trees. A group of singers from Colorado were there on a mission trip and, when we approached the door, we heard English. We found a place to sit toward the back. After we sang many songs both in German and English, we heard the man up front saying something about guests. As he looked back at me, I raised my hand timidly. Then, he asked us to stand and tell our names. I said we were thankful that one of their members had invited us. He asked us to come up front and tell the IKEA story.

Following the worship, we met Wolfgang, one of the elders, who invited us to come home for lunch with the singers. If you have taken Henry Blackaby's *Experiencing God*, you will understand when I say it was a God thing. As we got to know each other, Wolfgang shared how he had prayed for years for God to send workers. He offered to help us and our friends with visas.

Wolfgang and his wife were in their sixties, retired and ready to serve the Lord full-time. He held evangelistic discipleship classes in their home and promoted outreach and discipleship wherever he could. He said we were an answer to prayer. When we told him that one of the team's families was arriving that week, he offered his upstairs apartment for them to stay in until

they found a permanent place to live. The Lord was sure directing our path in ways we had never expected.

It was time to turn in our rental car, and we needed to do
that at the Munich Airport. We needed to turn it in because it
was a car that came from Paris. Then, we would rent one that
would stay in Germany. The lady at the rental office told us she
did not have the size we wanted but would rent us a larger one
for the same price. It turned out to be a new black Mercedes
with tinted windows. We needed a car, but we weren't sure how
it would look for a couple of missionaries driving such a luxuri-
ous one. We would also learn that it might cause a stir with the
police.

We continued doing errands to help our team, driving back
and forth through little towns. One night, as we drove through
a town, we were pulled over by the police. They walked around
the car and I rolled down the window. They said there was no
problem and we could continue. We must have looked like a
member of the Mafia driving that car!

We soon had our own car and the German law required that
within six months, drivers must pass the written test. It could
be taken in English, but we also had to pass a CPR class that was
only offered in German. David had taken CPR classes over the
years in the United States, so with his help we both passed the
class in German.

We had become acquainted with a lady who had an outreach
to the many refugees in Germany. She invited us to come for
lunch one day along with an Iranian couple and their son who
were refugees. The young man was an English teacher from Iran
and spoke good English. After lunch, we took a walk in the park
and David walked with the young man. He asked David a lot
of questions including questions about being a Christian. The
next time we saw the couple was when we went to sit in on the
missionary's German as a Second Language class followed by a
worship service. When our Iranian friend saw David, he told

the missionary that he wanted to talk with him about becoming a Christian. They went off into another room where David proceeded to walk him through a Gospel tract in English and Farsi. When David got to the end of the tract, he asked, "Is there any reason why you would not want to pray and ask Jesus to come into your heart?" The young Iranian paused and thought, and then said he would like to invite Jesus in. They prayed, and he received Jesus. Then, he asked David if he would show his wife the way to becoming a Jesus follower. David agreed and the next thing he knew the man was off to find his wife. The two of them returned. The wife did not speak any English, so her husband was translating. But soon, he took the tract from David and proceeded to go through it with her. He asked her to pray and the two prayed in Farsi. Praise the Lord! Our missionary friend later introduced the couple to someone who went to a Farsi-speaking church nearby. We don't know any more details but we look forward to seeing them in heaven one day.

The mission team had settled into their new locations and our team leader finally located a new house in town. Of course, it needed a kitchen and lighting fixtures. David had worked as an electrician at our church in Atlanta, so he was able to install twenty-one lighting fixtures. Finally, everyone was settled in, but then we realized there was no plan about what we would now do. We should have known after our experience in Cyprus. The team leader was still a visionary with new visions each day. He said we could help coordinate a conference in Switzerland. Then, he suggested we go to Rome and help a missionary there. Rome was one of seven Western European target cities for this project. Rome at that time had the largest mosque in Europe holding 5,000 Muslims.

As directed, we went to Interlaken, Switzerland, to arrange a conference for all the missionaries and their families who were associated with the project. Then on to Rome where we spent some time assisting the missionary there. We were invited to come back on a permanent basis. It didn't seem to matter to our leader that a lot of money had been spent on putting in a kitchen and lighting fixtures in our German apartment that we were now vacating. He himself would also move after doing the same in Dachau. We could see mission dollars going down the drain because of poor planning and no concrete leadership.

We moved to Rome to work with a missionary couple who had previously been in one of the communist countries. They had left that country because the wife claimed the children had been molested by a nanny. We were soon to learn that the wife was obsessed with claiming sexual molestation of her children. Now, the claim was against a nun where her children went to school. We were very careful never to be alone with any of the children. We were not available to babysit for the couple.

Again, we rented an apartment and had to put in the kitchen. Off to the Rome IKEA to purchase the cabinets and everything needed. We had a car furnished by the mission organization, so we thought we could take most everything with us. A young man named James, who we met in the parking lot, offered to help with the heavy items. I will never forget the scene. Cabinets loaded in the car with room for me, the driver. David was laying on the floorboard in the back with cabinets in the rest of the space. Before we drove away, we asked James if he could come when our moving truck arrived from Germany and help unload.

Later, we learned that the Pope invited young men from around the world to come to the Great Jubilee of 2000. After the Jubilee, many did not return to their home country but defected and stayed in Rome as illegals. That was the case for James and his friends from Bangladesh. One day, we were down near the Roman Forum with James and suddenly he bolted away. Then we saw a policeman and realized James was frightened because he was an illegal. Rome was also filled with gypsies who had come from other countries. We learned that most made their living as pickpockets. We had been warned to watch out for them on the subways. They would pretend to be carrying a baby covered by a blanket. The blanket would hide their activity of opening fanny packs and stealing anything they could find quickly. One day, when the subway stopped at a station, two policemen poked their heads in and warned all to watch their personal items. We had purchased some leather coats like most Italians wore, so we would blend in and not look like American tourists. David and I had a code word to alert each other when we suspected pickpockets near us. "Quarter back" on left or right, which ever applied.

While in Rome, we attended the Rome Baptist Church located near the Pantheon. Since it was so close one Sunday after church, we walked over to look at one of the best-preserved buildings from ancient Rome. It was completed in AD 125 during the reign of Hadrian. You would think you were stepping back 2,000 years looking at a building that is virtually intact and exhibits the genius work of Roman architects of that era.

Rome Baptist Church was a multicultural, English-speaking body of believers. They were committed to proclaiming the Good News and reaching out to the community. We were invited to develop and conduct a two-week evangelism training. It was a delight to facilitate this class and meet so many believers from different countries.

We continued our friendship with James, and he invited us over to his apartment where we met many more young men from Bangladesh. Life was difficult in their country and at that time the annual income was $300. That is, if one could get a job with 60% unemployment. We really liked these guys and we started a Bible study in their apartment. One day, they invited us to come for dinner. When we arrived, they had a small table set for two. They did not eat but served us a wonderful chicken dinner. It was so humbling because we knew they were spending money on us when they were going without. Later, when we departed Rome, we left them all our clothes except what we were wearing on the plane.

The missionary wife turned her husband's heart against us and, before we knew it, we were being dismissed. We called a counselor with the mission organization who came and talked with all of us individually. The missionary couple were not willing to meet with us and discuss their issues. We were to learn in a few years that that family was back in the US and no longer in missions.

We were there in Rome and needed to leave. No one seemed to care how we would go about moving back to the States. But God did. One day, we were down near the Coliseum and a piece of paper blew into our path. We reached down and picked it up. It was a flyer for a company that specialized in transporting people and their luggage to the airport. God never fails! Here was our direction to get our seventy-pound suitcases and us to the airport. "Trust in the Lord with all your heart, and do not lean on your own understanding. In all your ways acknowledge Him, and He will make straight your paths." (Psalm 3:5–6)

The day we left Rome went smoothly with the company on the flyer. When we checked in at the airport, we were surprised when the agent upgraded us to first class. A gift from the Lord. As we headed toward Naples, we reflected on a poem by Florence White Willett.[3]

> I thank You for the friends who've failed
> To meet my soul's deep needs;
> They've driven me to the Savior's feet
> Upon His love to feed.
> I'm grateful too, through all life's way
> No one could satisfy.

---

3. Ruth Myers with Warren Myers, *31 Days of Praise: Enjoying God Anew* (Multnomah Publishers, Colorado Springs, CO, 1994).

And so, I've found in You alone
My rich, my full supply!

CHAPTER SIX

Back to Naples

David and I returned to the United States in February 2001 after completing nine mission assignments over the past fifteen years. We had been moving in and out of the country with seventy-pound suitcases. The world would change on September 11, 2001, and places we had been were no longer safe.

Arriving back in Naples, we walked right into one of those storms of life. Storms will come whether you expect them or not. They are usually a big surprise and sometimes they knock you off your feet. I can't help reflecting on Matthew 14, the time Jesus sent His disciples to the other side of the sea. They had just been a part of one of Jesus' miracles of feeding five thousand. It must have been a high point in their lives. They saw Jesus take five loaves and two fish and feed all the people. They were part of collecting the twelve baskets of leftovers.

Now, Jesus told them to get in their boat and go before Him to the other side, while He dismissed the crowds. Jesus went to pray, and He knew that His disciples were going to face a storm. No surprise to Jesus! Charles Spurgeon once said, "I have learned to kiss the wave that throws me against the Rock of Ages." Like Beth Moore has said, "Faith is not believing in my own unshakable believe. Faith is believing an unshakable God when everything in me trembles and quakes."

> "The steadfast love of the Lord never ceases; His mercies never come to an end; they are new every morning; great is Your faithfulness. 'The Lord is my portion, therefore I will hope in Him.'" (Lamentations 3:22–24)

I will not go into the details of the storm we walked through, but I encourage every person reading this to pause and talk with the Lord about the hurt that they may have carried for years. Forgive the offender and thank the Lord that He took up your cause. Praise Him that the evil one could not thwart the plans that the Lord had for you. That He has blessed you beyond all you could ask or think. That He alone cares, protects you, and leads you in triumphant through the storms of life.

I had just turned sixty-two and qualified for Social Security if I wanted to take it and get a lesser paying job. That meant I could only earn so much, or I had to pay a Social Security penalty on extra earnings. Or I could wait until sixty-five, but that meant I needed to get a good paying job now. Either way, I wouldn't get medical insurance benefits until sixty-five. I interviewed for both kinds of jobs and I got really frustrated. I cried out to God one day, "Why don't you just write it on the wall like in the Book of Daniel?" A few days went by and I drove up to the Bank of America ATM. Yep, there it was, written on the bank wall on a flyer. The bank was asking for bank tellers, part-time with full medical benefits. I interviewed and became a bank teller for twenty hours a week with health benefits for both of us. David got a job at a Lee County Library as a page working the same twenty hours a week.

We had time now to get back to playing golf. One day, after we played a round at Country Creek, we saw an open house sign.

We stopped to look at the attached villa and started crunching the numbers. It looked like we could sell our present condo and move to this golfing community and play golf. The golf fee for members was low at that time. The move went quickly and, the next year, we played one hundred rounds of golf. We each got a hole in one, the second for me but twenty years apart.

Turning sixty-five meant that I could work as much as I wanted and still draw Social Security. Since we had served so many years on the mission field, we needed to save some funds for later years. The IRS was allowing for extra funds to go into an IRA at that time. I left the bank and did some Kelly Girl assignments. One day, they assigned me to a job at a condo in Pelican Landing. The husband of a hardworking realtor had insisted that she needed an assistant, and he asked Kelly Girl to send some candidates for him to interview. He chose me and I went to work for his wife.

After working for a few weeks, she encouraged me to get my real estate license. She paid for the training, gave me time during work to study, and paid for the exam. At the age of sixty-five, I got my license and passed the test the first time. Being a licensed personal assistant allowed me to answer all the client's questions, just like my realtor boss.

My boss had a friend who was in real estate and brought her on board. The new gal in the office did not like me and soon influenced my boss to fire me. A shock! My emotions were whirling. Condemnation set in. I wished I could just blow a whistle and stop the mental debating in my head. I wished I could stop and tell myself that God is in control and He is working out His plan for me. I was headed for a tremendous blessing and didn't know it.

John Piper wrote, "Romans 8:32 is a precious friend. The promise of God's future grace is simply overwhelming. But all-important is the foundation: I have called it the logic of heaven. Here is a place to stand against all obstacles. God did not spare His own Son! Therefore! Therefore! The logic of heaven! Therefore, how much more will He not spare any effort to give us all that Christ died to purchase—all things, all good, and all bad working for our good! It is as sure as the certainty that He loved His Son!"

I went over to the Bonita Springs Realtor Association Office and inquired if they knew of anyone wanting a licensed personal assistant. They said that a man named Jim had called, and they gave me his telephone number. I met with Jim and his son-in-law, Dan, for an interview.

They were followers of Jesus. They had just moved into their real estate office and showed me the boxes. They explained that they would both be listing and selling, and my job was to keep things organized. This turned out to be the best job I had ever had. Working for believers who were faithful to their calling makes for a fun and fulfilling job. At that time, I did not realize the part Dan would play in my life.

During the two years I worked for them, they invested in many properties. The real estate bust came in 2007 and they could no longer afford me. God, however, never misses a beat. We had flown to Texas to visit my youngest son. He and his family had been living in a small ranch house for ten years and were looking for something larger. David and I were having the discussion about what to do when we were older. We wanted to be together but did not know if we would be physically able to take care of each other. We had started exploring assisted living facilities.

One morning at breakfast, we sat around the table and talked about our plans for the future. One of us suggested that we might think about doing something together. My son suggested that perhaps he could have a home built with a section for us. We started making a list of the what ifs about living together. We thought we had all the bases covered. My son and daughter-in-law found a builder who would adjust a home plan to meet all our needs.

We went home and began selling the two properties we owned. We were able to sell one at top of the market but the rental property we finally sold for the mortgage left on it. We gifted my son several thousands of dollars and agreed to pay him a monthly rent. He agreed to take care of us for the rest of our lives. In fact, they changed their will to reflect this agreement.

He wanted us to come to Texas as soon as we could so we could help oversee the construction of the house. He sold his house and rented a house large enough for all of us as we waited the completion of our new home. As construction progressed, we all went over one day with markers and wrote Scripture on the studs. David and I wrote the following:

> "Blessed be the God and Father of our Lord Jesus Christ, the Father of mercies and God of all comfort, who comforts us in all our affliction, so that we may be able to comfort those who are in any affliction, with the comfort with which we ourselves are comforted by God." (2 Corinthians 1:3–4)

I remember standing where the bay window would soon be, looking out into the backyard, thinking that one or both of us might die in this room. A few years later, David would take his last breath there.

> "For if we have been united with Him in a death like His, we shall certainly be united with Him in a resurrection like His. We know that our old self was crucified with Him in order that the body of sin might be brought to nothing, so that we would no longer be enslaved to sin. For one who

has died has been set free from sin." (Romans 6:5–7)

"I have been crucified with Christ. It is no longer I who live, but Christ who lives in me. And the life I now live in the flesh I live by faith in the Son of God, who loved me and gave Himself for me." (Galatians 2:20)

These two were favorite passages for David and me. Years before, when I was in a Christ-centered counseling internship at Grace Fellowship in Atlanta, I began to understand the exchanged life and shared it with David.

Watchman Nee[4] in his book, *The Normal Christian Life*, wrote, "We think of the Christian life as a 'changed life,' but it is not that. What God offers us is an 'exchanged life,' a 'substituted life,' and Christ is our Substitute within." And, in Galatians 2:20: "It is no longer I who live, but Christ who lives in me . . ." This life is not something which we ourselves have to produce. It is Christ's own life reproduced in us.

"And we know that for those who love God all things work together for good, for those who are called according to His purpose. For those whom He foreknew He also predestined to be conformed to the image of His Son, in order that He might be the firstborn among many brothers." (Romans 8:28–29)

Most of the time this verse is best understood when we look back. When we are in the midst of trials or hard times, it may be difficult to see what good will come from it.

---

4. Watchman Nee, *The Normal Christian Life*.

The house was complete, and we all moved in. It was a comfortable place to live with family just on the other side of the wall. During the next four years, we spent about 25% of the time in Texas and the rest in Southwest Florida. Another son had a condo in Estero, Florida, and only used it about three times a year. He graciously let us stay there. It was an area where we had lived for several years and had many friends there. I remember one of the summers we were in Texas the temperature hit over 100 for so many days that it broke an all-time record. We went back to Florida to cool off.

One year, during our time in Florida, we went to Italy's Amalfi Coast for eighteen days. It was a Road Scholar trip and a celebration of David's eightieth birthday. That would be our last overseas trip. I am so glad we went when we were both healthy.

David and Dava in Amalfi, Italy

CHAPTER SEVEN

"Help," My World Is Shaking

O ver thirty years ago, David and I promised "in sickness and in death" and now things were happening that brought that promise to reality. I loved and adored my wonderful husband. He was so wise and trusted the Lord in everything. I depended on him so much. I listened to his suggestions and directions and obeyed with all my heart. But I started to question his directions.

David usually was the copilot with me doing the driving. His directions about where to turn were not as accurate as they used to be. I struggled with listening to my husband versus ignoring his directions and going the way I believed it should be. But that's not all that concerned me. Some of our daily events had begun to scare me. I did not know how to handle them. I didn't know if these were normal aging events or early signs of more serious mental illnesses, i.e., dementia or Alzheimer's. I knew David's heart did not operate properly. Perhaps, his brain might not be getting all the oxygen it needed. As a wife, I felt almost like I was betraying my husband to even talk with anyone about his memory issues, etc.

David had not been remembering to do daily hygiene tasks like brushing his teeth and shaving. One evening, I asked him if he had brushed his teeth that day and he said he had not remembered to do it. He wanted me to remind him of these things, but I felt it was quite demeaning to tell my husband to brush his teeth. I tried to be a good helpmate, so I made small cards and we discussed the things that he would need to do each day. I wrote one word on each card: *Teeth, Shaving, Shower,* etc. We agreed these cards would stay on the table and when he completed a task, he would turn the card over. Then, I only had to ask him how his cards were going each day. He seemed happy with the arrangement.

But the love of my life seemed to be having a difficult time. He spilled the V8 juice he was carrying on the way to the bathroom. I heard him say, "Oh, no, David." Later, when I went in the bathroom it was on the bathtub, toilet base, sink, cupboard, door, and doorjamb.

We were having the carpet cleaned. We had a large coffee table that needed to be moved so the cleaner could do a good job around that area. We sat in the den and discussed a plan to push that table in front of the window since that area was cleaner and wouldn't need as much care. A few minutes later, we were in the living room and he asked, "Where are we going to put the coffee table?"

He showered one morning and came out of the bathroom naked and stood in the doorway looking confused. I asked what was wrong, and he said he was looking for his clothes. He had left them before showering on top of the TV that was within three feet of him. He didn't seem to remember. He looked at them and said he needed undershorts and socks before he put those clothes on. He went into the bedroom and was in there quite a while, so I checked on him. He was sitting on the side of the bed with his undershorts and socks on. When I asked him what he was doing, he said he was trying to think about which leg to put in his other shorts first. He continued to be very disoriented for several hours. While we ate lunch on the lanai, he was quiet and very much isolated within himself. I asked him if he would turn on the overhead fan and while up to bring me my sunglasses. He got up, stumbled, and sat down in a living room chair. He couldn't seem to remember what he was after. He stumbled again and I had him sit back down. When I asked him why he was getting up, he replied, "To take another bite of dinner." After resting for a moment, I had him come back to the chair on the lanai. We decided to have a Ghirardelli chocolate. A few moments after that, he seemed to come back to reality. He acknowledged that he may have done too much physical labor and he thought the chocolate was what helped. He wanted another piece, which he ate. He seemed to be better mentally. Go figure. What do you think? Did the antioxidant help his mental state?

David usually got up to go to the bathroom during the night and I slept through it. One night, he woke me up while he was sitting on the side of the bed. He said he could not stand. I got up and helped him up and he could walk. The next night the same thing happened.

The next day was the carpet cleaning and, because I had bad knees, I asked David to vacuum under the bed. He did and then he was mentally out of it. At first, I thought that he might have had a stroke and I gave him the FAST ministroke test, which he passed.

F: Face drooping. Ask the person to smile and see if one side is drooping.
A: Arm weakness. Ask the person to raise both arms.
S: Speech difficulty.
T: Time to call 911!

We had been spending the winter in my son's condo in Florida and did not have a family doctor. The day after the carpet cleaning, we made an appointment to see a doctor. We had to fill out some forms for the appointment the following day. I filled them out, but David had a difficult time signing his name. He knew his name, but just couldn't seem to write it. The next day, we saw Dr. Sherman and she ordered a CAT scan of the brain, an ultrasound of the neck arteries, an echo of the heart, an X-ray of the lungs, and blood tests. She was going to be away for the Christmas holidays, so we could not get a follow-up appointment until January 3rd.

I had been getting more and more concerned about David's mind and memory and I kept it to myself. I realized that I needed a confidante. I felt a need to share some of the daily events that were scaring me, and I did not know how to handle. I still didn't know if these were normal aging events or if some might be early signs of more serious illnesses. As a wife, I continued to feel like I was betraying my husband to even talk to someone about his memory, incontinence, and shuffling walk. I was seeing a need and yet afraid to share it with anyone except God. I finally reached out to a family member to be my confidante. After she prayed about it, she declined. I felt so alone!

David would sit with his head down when someone was talking to him. He had difficulty hearing and I had to get his attention first and repeat everything. Could this be old age? His personality seemed to change gradually. He seemed like he was in a fog and even described that as a feeling. Often, he was confused.

We had been avid bridge players for years and now he had difficulty playing bridge, so we stopped playing. I had to monitor him constantly. I was afraid he would get lost when out for a walk. He walked very slowly with his head down, shoulders rounded forward, and wore the heels of his shoes off from shuffling. His balance got worse. He began using walls and furniture for balance, then a walker. Eye-to-hand coordination seemed to be off. He knocked over a glass or cup at most meals. He felt fatigued, confused, forgetful, and had difficulty at times completing sentences.

Urinary problems developed and he had an urgency and frequent accidents. For example, during a one-and-a-half-hour concert we attended he had to get up and go to the restroom six times. During each trip to the restroom he said he had a good quantity of flow. He had to wear Depends most of the time when he left home. Could this be age-related problems?

When he went to the grocery store, he would go to the bathroom before leaving home. When he got to the store one mile away, he would go again, and another one to two times during shopping before returning home. There were times he would get up six times during the night and I would find him wandering in the kitchen. I felt like I slept with one eye open. David was very tired and often dozed while sitting.

On January 3, we went to the follow-up doctor's visit that ended up lasting over twenty-four hours. Dr. Sherman panicked when she listened to David's heartbeat. Although it hadn't changed since she had listened to it at the last visit. She insisted he go next door to the hospital emergency. We did and David was admitted. The next day, the cardiologist that had been assigned came in and said, "What doctor panicked and put you in here?" We were no further ahead on solving David's real problem.

We opted to fire Dr. Sherman. David, who was from Atlanta, said he should have known she would be trouble since General Sherman burned Atlanta. He still had his sense of humor! Upon discharge from the hospital, we were given the names of a couple of primary doctors who were taking new patients. An appointment was made, but we couldn't get in until mid-February.

Six weeks later the new doctor ordered an MRI of the brain. He wanted David to see a neurologist and have an evaluation at the Memory Clinic. Because we had lived overseas for so many years, I always got a copy of tests to carry with me. I got a copy of the MRI and arranged a date for the evaluation at the Memory Clinic. The neurologist could not see us until late March.

Still, no one to talk with and David's symptoms were getting worse. I sent out a prayer request to several people describing his symptoms and asking for prayer. One of my cousins, who was a retired school nurse, emailed back. "When I heard David's symptoms it rang a bell. A few weeks ago, I read an article about NPH—normal pressure hydrocephalus. This is a little known and an often missed disease. David seems to have some of the symptoms. Here are a couple of websites you might want to look at. There are others you can google. I'm sure you have an excellent neurologist, but it might not hurt to ask about this if you think the symptoms might be similar, just to be sure he has thought of this and ruled it out. Good luck and will keep you both in our thoughts and prayers."

I ran to find my copy of the MRI report. Yes, same thing, normal pressure hydrocephalus. When I had previously read the report, I thought *normal* meant "normal." Now, I began to research the disease. I found an article published in *The Nurse Practitioner,*[5] "Normal pressure hydrocephalus (NPH) is often an unrecognized cause of dementia symptoms, and can be reversible with appropriate diagnosis and treatment, specifically ventriculoperitoneal (VP) shunting. It has been estimated that 375,000 Americans misdiagnosed with dementia or Parkinson's disease have symptoms that are caused by normal pressure hydrocephalus. Some experts suggest that as many as 6% of nursing home residents may have NPH." The article noted that it could be helped with a brain shunt if indeed it was NPH. The article also listed the clinical manifestations as follows:

---

5. Christine Byrd, "Normal Pressure Hydrocephalus: Dementia's Hidden Cause," *The Nurse Practitioner* 31, No. 7 (July 2006): 28–35.

Clinical Triad of NPH

Clinical Manifestations	Characterized By:
Gait disturbance	Wide-based, shuffling gait Difficulty picking up feet Problems with stairs, curbs Instability with turning Frequent falls
Dementia symptoms	Short-term memory deficits Loss of interest in daily activities Difficulty with routine tasks Lack of spontaneity in actions and verbal response Slow processing of information Problems with retention of language skills
Urinary incontinence	Urinary frequency and urgency (early sign) Urinary incontinence (late sign)

Searching the Internet, I noticed that Florida Orlando Hospital had a three-day in-hospital test to determine if a shunt would be beneficial. I learned more about the disease when I called and talked with the hospital NPH Coordinator. I called the NPH Association and they said that there were no doctors in our immediate area that do the three-day test. They also confirmed that many in nursing homes who have been diagnosed with Alzheimer's have NPH and it can be corrected.

By this time, David had his appointment with the Memory Clinic and the results were back. No dementia, not even mild dementia, but above normal memory limits for his age group. Wow! The report mentioned that NPH should be checked out.

I found a local Alzheimer Network and searched their website. There was no mention of NPH, so I made an appointment to meet with the director personally. Bottom line—they really didn't have any information. They told me that they had known a few people who had had a shunt and it didn't solve the problem. They were completely unaware of the three-day in-hospital test. At the end of our conversation, I think they may have been more aware of what to look for, but sad to say they said it is all up to the local neurologist to diagnose and test.

Finally, the day came for the neurologist appointment. Prior to the appointment, I called his office and confirmed they had received the memory evaluation. I asked about the MRI and they had not received it. I said, "You probably would like the actual pictures and not just the report." Yes, they did. I retrieved the MRI film and a copy of the report and carried the large, purple envelop into the neurologist's office.

The neurologist greeted us and began to yawn. He told us about his late night with his adult children and he was so tired. He looked at David and said, "What are we doing here with a memory evaluation in the upper limits? You don't have dementia." I sensed he had not looked at the MRI report that I had in my hand. I asked him about the other things on the MRI report and he said, "What are they? Let me see your copy." He looked at the report then latched on to NPH and asked David if he had incontinence and if he shuffled. Now he had his diagnosis. He said David needed a have a cisternogram. We said we would get back to him. He walked out to the reception area with us and he neither looked at the MRI films nor even acknowledged the large, purple envelop that I was carrying.

I rushed home and called the Florida Orlando Hospital. They said the cisternogram the neurologist prescribed was outdated and nonconclusive. I called the NPH Association in California and they said the same thing. I called some local neurologists and neurosurgeons' offices and learned they also used this outdated test. No one locally did the three-day in-hospital testing to be sure a shunt was needed. I understood there were only six hospitals in the United States that did this type of testing. My mission now was to get David to Orlando for the three-day in-hospital test.

The Florida Orlando Hospital's Neuroscience Institute had an amazing team working on this disease and doing research. David had a steady stream of medical personnel during the evaluation. I estimated thirty different doctors, nurses, technicians, including resident doctors, medical students, student nurses, and physical therapy students who were involved in the evaluation. It was quite an international team with two Iranians (the internal medicine doctor and a nurse), one Pakistani resident doctor, some Filipino nurses, a nurse born in India, as well as Americans and those from the Caribbean.

The Neuroscience Institute only took two patients for this evaluation per week. They placed the two patients in private rooms, one on each side of the nurse's station, because many of those being evaluated were confused and some without family members to be with them. I heard that some had come from other countries for this evaluation.

I cannot say enough about this hospital in downtown Orlando. It covers many blocks. It was founded in 1908 when some Seventh Day Adventists came to Orlando and felt the need for a medical facility that not only met physical needs, but spiritual needs as well. Staff members were assigned to a small team that got together daily before their shift started to pray.

Our contact from my first phone call to the hospital about David's problem was with the NPH Clinical Research Coordinator. She had graduated with a nursing degree and had a biomed degree before taking this position. She orchestrated this program and was the facilitator for the monthly meeting. Each month, all the medical personnel who were involved with NPH patient evaluations met to discuss each of the patients. The group rated each patient for shunt benefits: probable, possible, or unlikely.

David was tested for syphilis and it was negative. I asked why they run this test? They were looking for dormant antibodies of syphilis among the aging. It was prevalent fifty plus years ago. David remembered being warned in the Navy about the disease.

Lying dormant, it can cause problems in the aging. They told us that a person with neurosyphilis had damage to the spinal cord, which gradually worsened. Eventually, the affected person would lose the ability to walk. General paresis was marked by damage to the brain cells, which might cause paralysis as well as seizures and a deteriorating mental state. With this condition, parts of the brain and spinal cord become inflamed, causing a wide range of neurological issues. They were doing research to determine if people diagnosed with Alzheimer's and dementia had syphilis antibodies.

David's NPH evaluation began at 5:00 a.m. with an MRI of the brain. David had had a brain MRI recently that showed ventricular enlargement and possible NPH, but this one was looking for more specific information, such as Evans ratio, velocity (more fluid will move faster), fluid amount, flow, ventricular enlargement, etc. Following the MRI, he was taken to his hospital room. They started an IV to nourish him.

Then, people began coming in to get their baseline information. He had a physical therapy team evaluating his gait, turning, balance, ability to sit and stand, etc. He had an internal medicine geriatric doctor and his team examining him and ordering blood tests. The neuropsychologist came and interviewed both of us together about David, and then he met with David alone and gave him an evaluation test to establish a baseline. The NPH Clinical Research Coordinator was involved to make sure everything was happening and answering all our questions. Nurses were monitoring David throughout the day.

Once everyone had their baseline, David was taken to have the *lumbar drain* put in. It was described as about the size an eighteen-inch piece of angel hair pasta. Once inserted, the doctor put a couple of stitches to keep it in place. It had a shutoff valve attached outside which later got hooked to a small receiving container on an IV stand. After collection of 17 ml, the container valve was opened and emptied into a bag much like an IV bag. David's *CSF*, his spinal brain fluid, was drained every two hours night and day for forty-eight hours, a total of 325 ml. He felt no pain and couldn't even feel it draining. He had to lay flat for about twenty minutes after so he wouldn't have any reactions. He never got a headache. Some samples were taken from the bag for testing and culturing, to make sure there was no infection. The draining mimics what a brain shunt does to see if David improved from the reduced fluid in his brain. After the lumbar drain was inserted, an antibiotic was fed through the IV every eight hours throughout the stay to prevent any infection. David had two poles, the drain stand and the IV stand, to pull if he wanted to walk to the bathroom.

The next day continued with quite a lot of activity as medical personnel returned to follow up and make sure David was doing okay. We always had lots of questions for them and they patiently answered without us feeling like they needed to rush off.

The Clinical Research Manager visited with us and explained about the research. She explained again how many people are misdiagnosed with Alzheimer's disease and might have normal pressure hydrocephalus. NPH was often mistaken for Parkinson's or attributed to the effects of aging. Typically, it affects adults over fifty-five, so the number of cases was expected to grow as the boomers age. David agreed to be part of the NPH research project over the next five years.

I was staying at a hotel across the street and the hospital supplied a shuttle between hotel–hospital and vice versa. I got a good ten-hour sleep each night. I called David before I left the hotel the second morning and his voice and greeting were more alive.

The recliner in his room was broken so I just propped pillows behind me, and it wasn't too bad. I felt there were more important things for nurses to do than get me a new chair. When I arrived at the hospital on the second morning, I learned that David dragging his two poles had moved that large recliner out into the hall before they caught him in the act. This was a sign of the "old persistent David" I knew before. He moved about the room better and could get up and down better.

After three days in the hospital, they had drained fluid from his spine every two hours for a total of eleven ounces. He was a different person. He was cheerful, laughing, joking, and more alert, held his head up and was involved in conversation. I could see a big difference. His urination was not so frequent, nor did he have an urgency to urinate. He wasn't dozing off like he had been doing even during lunch one day.

Thursday was the day everyone came back to take a new evaluation so they could compare it with their baseline. The physical therapist saw a difference. One test they did was asking David to walk a certain distance, turn, and come back. They counted the number of steps, so they could see the difference between the baseline and the final evaluation. They felt his speed, initiation of steps, and balance were better. They made a recommendation for him to have ongoing physical therapy for balance and strengthening.

The geriatrics internal medicine doctor was Persian and we loved him. He, together with his entourage (totaling about six), would come in or one of them would stop by. A female resident from Pakistan was a frequent visitor attending David. Even a first-year medical student was involved. This group, headed by the internal medicine doctor, placed orders for David to be hooked up to a heart monitor, have several bladder scans after he urinated to make sure the bladder was emptying, and multiple blood tests.

The neuropsychologist felt on the retest that David had done better than the base. He had to enter all the test information into the computer to get the real analysis. The neurosurgeon who heads the NPH program and research came in and removed the drain. He asked us lots of questions about what symptoms we first noticed and when, etc. He was a delightful man of about sixty years old with lots of energy. He was in favor of doing David's shunt, but wanted to wait until after the evaluation meeting process to have each person's input in the report. We were now looking forward to a shunt being placed to drain off all the extra fluid David was producing. David had probably had NPH for several years and had been gradually getting worse. David was eight years older than me and the aging thing was new to us, we discounted a lot to "normal aging". We were realizing that it was not all normal aging, but NPH. The three-day evaluation gave us a sample of what a shunt would do. I felt like I got the David I knew back again.

We headed home realizing that the evaluation draining relieved symptoms, but we had been told that as fluid builds up over time, the old symptoms would come back within days. David began to have difficulty walking which showed us how quickly David could revert to his previous condition without the shunt.

During the next days, his walk became more unsteady. He went around holding onto walls and furniture. Now, he knew it was difficult to walk; before, he would say he was OK. He remembered how good he felt after the three-day fluid draining and how well he could walk. Incontinence didn't seem to be a problem.

When David stood up from sitting, he had a difficulty lifting his feet off the floor. Then he was able to walk with a cane. He felt tired at breakfast and said, "I feel so sluggish." The next day continued with his energy level low, he walked slow and guarded. I could see confusion and forgetfulness coming back and more memory problems appearing. He was sitting with head down again.

David had progressively deteriorated as the CSF built up. His walking was becoming more difficult. His legs felt weak and his muscles hurt. He had more difficulty getting out of a chair. His mental functions were impaired with the fluid interrupting brain signals. Incontinence had returned with frequency and urgency.

I learned that the brain usually has one ounce of this fluid. In David's hospital evaluation, they drained off 20 ml every two hours (0.676 oz) for a total of 325 ml (almost 11 oz) over a forty-eight-hour period. Once the shunt was placed, he would have continuous draining, and those symptoms should disappear. The brain shunt functions automatically, draining the fluid from the brain into the abdominal cavity.

During the next days, it appeared that the CSF was building up and causing the symptoms to appear within a few days of the lumbar draining. This was an additional signal that a shunt was needed. We decided we needed to get the shunt surgery done soon. I had to remember that David was eighty-one and I was not sure what the real eighty-one-year-old David would look like. The shunt would not roll back normal aging and make him ten years younger.

Brain shunt surgery was scheduled. The night before we met with the surgeon, he marked the area of the head where he would cut approximately three inches in the scalp. The valve would be implanted. Once cut, the surgeon would drill a small hole in the skull to insert a small piece of the tubing into the right ventricular of the brain. The tubing would go from the ventricular into the valve. An incision was made in the neck to pull the tubing down and to test the flow. Then an incision in the abdomen to bring the tubing down into the abdominal cavity where the CSF would drain and be absorbed. David had opted to enter the shunt research and an Integra Flow Regulating Valve–Mini was to be used. The surgery would take about an hour and he could be discharged the same day.

We arrived at the hospital at 6:00 a.m. for the 8:00 a.m. surgery. The surgery took an hour. David spent the day trying to wake up, had some liquids, and at about 6:00 p.m. he had a solid meal. He was in good spirits and giving out some dry humor to nurses. He did not seem to be in much discomfort—just a sleepy head. Getting up at 4:45 a.m. may have added to the tired feeling.

The early morning got to me, too. I was staying at a hotel nearby. He ate his dinner and was taken for his first walk by two nurses. I headed to the hotel for a good night's sleep, so I would be prepared to bring David from the hospital to the hotel for a few days. They kept him in recovery overnight and I picked him up by 9:00 a.m. to take him to the hotel.

The surgeon told me to get him out for dinner, walking, and as active as possible during the next few days. The shunt valve works differently when sleeping and idle versus walking and active. He said it will not be as dramatic a change as it was during the three-day evaluation. It will be a more gradual improvement.

David and Dava at dinner the day after the shunt was placed

The doctor had arranged for home health care to come to the hotel for two to three days to look at the wounds and change the dressings. Then, we would head home where the doctor had arranged for another week of home health care to monitor wounds. After seven to ten days, the stitches would be removed.

Back home. David was doing great with the brain shunt. All his symptoms went away after it was placed (no shuffling, dementia, incontinence). He had hiccups for three weeks probably because of the shunt being pulled down to the abdomen.

Prompting cards for daily hygiene were no longer needed and were thrown away. David was a team player and helped with household duties, etc. He drove himself to physical therapy where he was regaining his balance. He did grocery shopping and no longer needed to use the restroom while shopping. Incontinence was no longer a problem.

He developed a new challenge, a rectal prolapse. We saw a rectal surgeon and he explained that the rectal prolapse occurs when part of the large intestine's lowest section (rectum) slips outside the muscular opening at the end of the digestive tract (anus). The prolapsed rectum can cause fecal incontinence. He said that David had a partial prolapse and if David was his father, he would not do surgery at this time. He suggested that he eat small meals, low fat, high fiber, and lots of fruits, vegetables, water, and use Depends. He had to sit on the prolapsed rectum to make it go in, so it eliminated his daily walk.

Even with the rectal prolapse, David said, "I feel like without my neurosurgeon and Florida Orlando Hospital, I would have never been diagnosed properly." He said he had renewed enthusiasm, energy, and felt like he was fifteen years younger than his eighty-one years. "God gave me a new life." He interacted with his head up. His hearing was good and repeating was rarely necessary even when in another room. Now, he was like his old self: alert, joking, laughing, not so intense, and initiating conversation. His sense of humor was back.

We were able to go out for lunch, go on a weeklong cruise, and we were back to playing competitive duplicate bridge. God had restored David's well-being and gave him the gift of time.

CHAPTER EIGHT

Seek God in the Present

"Count it all joy, my brothers, when you meet trials of various kinds, for you know that the testing of your faith produces steadfastness. And let steadfastness have its full effect, that you may be perfect and complete, lacking in nothing." (James 1:2–4)

Myelodysplastic syndromes, also known as *MDS*, are a group of blood and bone marrow disorders. MDS is considered a type of cancer. In MDS, stem cells do not mature as expected. This causes an increase in the number of immature cells, called *blasts*, and abnormally developed cells, called *dysplastic cells*. Also, the number of healthy mature cells in the blood decreases, causing the bone marrow to work poorly or to stop working altogether. This means that there are fewer healthy red blood cells, white blood cells, and/or platelets.

Because of the decrease in healthy cells, people with MDS often have *anemia*, which is a low red blood cell count. They may also have *neutropenia*, which is a low white blood cell count, and *thrombocytopenia*, which is a low platelet count. In addition, dysplastic white blood cells and platelets may not work correctly. Also, the *chromosomes*, or long strands of genes, in the bone marrow cells may be abnormal.

Why am I providing all this information? It was information that I never had a clue about. Not until it became very personal. Not until David was diagnosed with MDS.

David had done so well with the brain shunt and we had returned to playing bridge and the other activities that we shared a love for. Follow-up with the neurosurgeon went well and he was not scheduled to go back again for months. The rectal prolapse was a daily struggle and soon would need surgery.

We continued to live in Florida and David saw the primary doctor frequently. The doctor would order blood tests. We got a call one day that David's platelets had dropped significantly. For years David had a low white blood count, but it was dropping too low. The primary doctor suggested we see a hematologist and we made an appointment with one.

When the hematologist had analyzed the recent blood test, he wanted to do a bone marrow test immediately. We opted to return to the Dallas area where David had consulted with a hematologist a few years ago. We made an appointment with that physician and headed back to Texas.

The first thing we did upon arriving in Texas was to see his hematologist who tested his low platelets, white blood cells, etc. He ordered a bone marrow test, and it showed David had myelodysplatic syndrome. MDS is more common with advancing age; most people are older than sixty years of age when diagnosed, although it can happen at any age. In most cases, the cause of MDS is unknown, but aging is associated with the accumulation of mutations in genes within bone marrow stem cells. MDS can lead to acute leukemia. Options—have some chemotherapy to suppress cell damage, but David chose not to do that since he felt good. He was just on the border of the intermediate stage, so he opted for supportive care. With MDS, the dangers are bleeding and/or infections. David's blood was monitored on a regular basis and he was given shots and/or transfusions as needed.

The brain shunt had been in for a year and worked great. We both forgot he even had it. His neurosurgeon in Orlando told him about a neurosurgeon located at the University of Texas at Southwestern. He said he taught neurosurgery and had a private practice. We saw him and all was well. He suggested David come back in a year.

We found a rectal surgeon. She had a different technique for dealing with the prolapse. It made sense to David. David gave the okay for surgery and it was scheduled. He would go in the hospital a day before surgery so they could evaluate and address his blood needs. We saw his cardiologist and David had a nuclear stress test for surgery clearance. He did fine and that doctor gave his okay. We got the okay from his neurosurgeon since his surgery would be laparoscopic and the brain shunt drain was in the abdomen cavity. David needed his blood values built up prior to surgery so we consulted with the hematologist to see how many white blood cell shots or other preventative measures he would need for the rectal surgery. The day before surgery, he received platelet transfusions, with additional post-operative transfusions after surgery as well.

David survived the rectal surgery with the help of three platelet transfusions. We continued to enjoy life together. Our bridge playing was now online. We each had a computer and could set up a table on a bridge site and play partners.

I was going to the pool to exercise with a free membership through SilverSneakers. I loved being able to shop at my favorite market, Sprouts. Loved being back with family just on the other side of the wall. We had redecorated our place with comfy leather recliners, a 47" LG Smart TV, new computer desks, some new lights, and electric-controlled blinds that cut out the hot Texas sun. David was a big Atlanta Braves fan and we got a subscription to the baseball channel. I got involved at the senior center and played mahjong once a week. I met new friends.

My knee problems had continued since I stepped the wrong way on the cobblestone streets of Pompeii. That was during our trip to the Amalfi area. We happened to have two doctors in our Road Scholar group who thought I might have torn my meniscus. They were right. Since returning from Italy, I had done quite well until I helped pack the car and drove back to Texas. I went to an orthopedic doctor at Baylor and loved him. The problem was on the inside of the knee where it was bone on bone with arthritis. The front part was worn and sometimes would catch. He gave me a shot to calm down the inflammation. He prescribed physical therapy so I could learn exercises that hopefully would help build thigh muscle and take pressure off the front. For the side problem, he had me fitted for a brace that would shift the kneecap to relieve the bone rubbing. A lady came to the house to fit me with a brace. She said I was fortunate to have my doctor since 95% of orthopedic doctors in this area go right to knee replacement. My doctor used all conservative measures before replacement. I liked that!

David continued to see his hematologist, and his numbers were dropping. His platelets got as low as one. We talked openly about death, and David was secure in his faith that when he took his last breath that he would be with Jesus. The day came when his hematologist talked with him about the low blood counts and suggested hospice. David opted for hospice at home on February 26 with the agreement that he could still have transfusions when necessary. He had one or two transfusions, but they would only increase his blood cells for a few days.

It had been eight months since we returned to Texas and David was getting weaker and weaker. Our two granddaughters, who had been home on spring break, were due to go back to college. We decided we would all go out for lunch at The Capital Grille in Dallas. We would celebrate my son's birthday, my birthday, and the girls returning to school after spring break. Most of all, we would celebrate David being able to go with us. This turned out to be David's last outing.

The girls returned to school. My son and daughter-in-law were pursuing a desire to move to Knoxville where her parents lived. My son had received permission from his employer to live there and keep his job. My daughter-in-law, who had become a nurse, was searching for a nursing job in that area. They had gone to Knoxville to check out housing and the job market. Everyone was out of the house for a week. I was alone caring for David with the help of hospice.

March 20th came, and David wanted to celebrate my birthday. He said he wanted lobster. I phoned in a take-out order and got him out of bed and to the table. He said he thought he was going to throw up. I grabbed a towel to catch it, but his stomach settled down. I made him promise not to move until I got back with the order. He seemed to enjoy some lobster but was exhausted and wanted to go back to bed.

It was rough days for the two of us. David fell backwards one evening. He escaped with a cut on his hand, but with hardly any platelets, he had lots of bruises on the back of his arms and butt. That ended his night trips to the bathroom. Hospice came to our rescue another night and left after 1 a.m. David seemed to decline during the next few days. He could no longer stand or walk by himself and I didn't have the strength to hold him up, so he was basically bedridden.

By the time my son and daughter-in-law returned from Tennessee I was exhausted. Hospice arranged for David to go to inpatient respite care for a few days. My daughter-in-law took him and went to see him over the weekend. I slept fifteen hours the first night and twelve the second. Three days later, the two of us picked him up. He had declined more over those days. He slept most of the day, but at night he was very restless and tried to get out of bed. The three of us worked as a team to make sure he was never alone day or night. An aide came five days a week to bed bathe him. The nurse was scheduled twice a week. We talked to her almost every day. My daughter-in-law was putting to practice the licensed RN degree she had received recently and gave David loving care. The hospice nurse estimated he did not have much more than a week to live.

Praise the Lord, he was not in pain. He knew us and we poured out our love for him with touches, back rubs, singing praise songs, words of comfort, feeding him all the foods he wanted like Oreo/Butterfinger Blasts, Blizzards, milkshakes, and homemade oatmeal raisin cookies, and made him feel as good as possible.

David and I lived in one large room that I guess you would call the mother-in-law quarters. When hospice brought in a single bed for David, our queen bed was pushed to the other side of the room. I slept just across the room from him. One eye open and alert. One night, the family sent me upstairs to bed in one of the girl's rooms while they took turns watching David to make sure he didn't try to get out of bed. We had been trying some of the meds hospice left for David to help him sleep at night, but we didn't have the doses perfected. We were all look-ing to God for strength during these last days while David was getting ready to go be with Jesus.

On Wednesday, March 26, David was interacting with us and called me "Little Dahlin'" as he usually did. David asked who that man was standing in the corner. We told him we didn't see any man. Later that day, he said, "I see a flock of schools." I heard him and asked if they were angels. He responded that it looked more like birds, white birds. I wondered if it could be doves. Months later, while reading in Revelation, I came across verse 17 in chapter 19 that said, "And I saw an angel standing in the sun; and he cried with a loud voice, saying to all the fowls that fly in the midst of heaven, 'Come and gather yourselves to-gether unto the supper of the great God . . .'" Apparently, David was seeing things that were preparing him to leave his earthly body. Many people tell similar stories of people seeing angels and men standing in the room as they approach their last days on earth.

Thursday was David's son Mike's birthday. I phoned Mike and put the phone to David's mouth, and he told Mike, "Happy Birthday." It was difficult for David to talk because his breathing was laborious. Those were the last words he said. Shortly after that, he was sedated and David went to be with the Lord at 7:30 a.m. on Friday, March 28, 2014.

God answered our prayers that he be taken home quickly and without pain. David lived twenty-one months after his shunt placement before going to be with the Lord from a bone marrow disease. God gave David a gift of life for those last months and gave David and me some special, beautiful moments.

CHAPTER NINE

Life after David

I had wonderful support during those early months of grieving from my son and daughter-in-law who I lived with in
Dallas. They said, "We are going to love you like you have
never been loved before." I thought that was such an amazing
statement. I felt their love.

Another son flew me to Florida for three weeks to stay in his
condo. I felt like a spoiled parent. During those three weeks, I
attended church at Covenant Naples. I had lived in this Florida
area full-time for about ten years until 2008. We had attended Covenant Naples mostly on Sunday nights when David was
well enough. Now, I got to attend Mary Ann Lee's class. She is
a gifted Bible teacher. Sitting under her teaching blessed me.
She has a special gift for making the Word of God come alive
and applicable for life today. We keep in touch. She is one of my
prayer warriors.

I was feeling refreshed from my time in Florida. I returned
to Texas where I continued to have knee problems. For three
years, I was David's caretaker and I had postponed some of my
own medical needs. I finally scheduled knee replacement.

David and I had read the Bible and prayed every morning
together, so I was missing not only my best friend, but my daily
prayer partner. My son gave me a copy of the book *A Praying*

Life, and it really changed my prayer life. It showed me how prayer is an intimate relationship with the Lord. I continued to learn more about how to live life through prayer.

I started praying for a Christian friend. One day, I was planning to play mahjong at a Jewish lady's house. I thought, "I'll go early and take myself out to lunch." I checked the route to Jen's house and there was a Jason's Deli on the way.

I picked up *A Praying Life* and headed for the restaurant. After ordering, I sat down at a table near the serving line. At the same time, a pesky fly also sat down, so I decided to move to another table. I chose one that was on the side looking out toward other tables. While I was eating, I noticed six ladies sitting at one table, and they were praying. Not just a "thank you for this food" prayer, but a prolonged time of prayer. It blessed me.

When I got ready to leave, I went by their table and held up *A Praying Life* and thanked them for praying in public. We struck up a conversation and I learned they were just going to start a Precept Bible Study the next week. The teacher, Margaret, was sitting at the end of the table and invited me to come to the study. I told them I was about to have bilateral knee replacement. We exchanged phone numbers.

I called Margaret before my surgery and we got together. We talked for about three hours and felt like we had known each other all our lives. We bonded as "best friends." I gave her a copy of *A Praying Life.* We got together several times. She has been a Bible teacher for about thirty years. She is a great encourager for me. And I believe the Lord has used me in her life. I stand amazed at how the Lord can answer prayer for a friend through a pesky fly.

Margaret gave her daughter-in-law a copy of *A Praying Life* and one to her son, a youth pastor in Alabama. She told me that her daughter-in-law was teaching *A Praying Life* at her church. Margaret just finished teaching a group of twenty women *A Praying Life* at her church in the Dallas area. That was indeed a divine appointment at Jason's Deli and an answer to several prayers.

About six months after David's homegoing, I had both knees replaced simultaneously. One surgeon on one knee and one on the other. Surgery was completed in one-and-a-half hours. During my stay in the hospital, I was given too much morphine and I suffered an overdose. The hospital staff called in their 911 to revive me. During that time, I threw a clot to the lung that, praise the Lord, dissolved.

I knew that after surgery I would not have a leg to stand on. LOL. I had done some research prior to surgery on where to go for in-house rehab. I was transferred from the hospital to the rehab facility where I stayed for two weeks. Then, I was sent home for in-home rehab for another four weeks. And, finally, I got to go to outpatient rehab. I regained 100% range of motion. Praise the Lord!

I continued to realize more than ever that I couldn't do life on my own. I asked God to show me how to do "Life after David." I told God that without David there was a void in my life and there was loneliness that even a room full of people couldn't fill. I missed the encouragement of my best friend and companion. Continually, I asked, "Lord, what is my purpose now? Where do I fit?" Day after day, I continued to pray that the Lord would show me what "Life after David" was like.

Even though David and I had once led our church's Tuesday night outreach and I knew how to share the Four Spiritual Laws with a nonbeliever, I felt inadequate. I started thinking about the changes in the culture around me and I began studying various worldviews. I began to realize we are surrounded by many different worldviews and forms of secularism. As Christians, so many of us have compartmentalized our lives, i.e., work life/church life/home life. I began studying these changes by taking the Ligonier R. C. Sproul online course "Christian Worldview versus Secularism." *Secularism* is the idea that all life must be judged by today's values. There is a real contrast between the Christian view of the world and the way the secularist views the world.

I listened to Francis Schaeffer on YouTube. I read portions of *Total Truth—Liberating Christianity from Its Cultural Captivity* by Nancy Pearcey. She was an associate of Francis Shaeffer and wrote, "Worldview is a window by which we view the world and decide (often subconsciously) what is real and important or unreal and unimportant." I listened to Ravi Zacharias and Alistair Begg speaking on the subject.

I had been involved in missions and evangelism for years, but the playing field had changed. The Good News message was the same, but the method needed to be different. I did not know how to share my faith with such a diverse and even hostile society. I knew how to present the Gospel, the Four Spiritual Laws, but did not know how to reach that point with someone in today's world. I felt unequipped to talk with people about Jesus. With this new awareness had come a desire for training on how to share Jesus in this upside-down world.

It is like I had my head in the sand and now I was seeing and hearing the secularist view all over the place. I went to a Newcomers' Coffee in Plano where each person was asked to share their "bucket list." After forty women had shared, one of the ladies wanted to sum it all up with a quote which stated that we don't need to search for meaning in life but "meaning of life is what you make it." I thought about Proverbs 16:9, "The mind of man plans his way, but the Lord directs his steps."

"The Robin and the Sparrow"
Said the robin to the sparrow,
"I should really like to know,
Why these anxious human beings
Rush about and worry so."
Said the sparrow to the robin,

"Friend I think that it must be,
That they have no Heavenly Father,
Such as cares for you and me."

—Elizabeth Cheney

I had 150,000 miles on my 2001 Honda. I began praying for a different car. After praying for a few weeks, I decided I really didn't need another car and scratched the request off my prayer list.

Truly, 2014 had been quite a year. In March, my husband David went to be with the Lord and, in October, I had both knees replaced at the same time. On November 29, once again I cried out to God, "I don't know how to do 'Life after David.'" I felt a void and loneliness. He was my best friend and companion. We did everything together. "Oh, Lord, what is my purpose? Where do I fit?"

The next day was Sunday and my son and daughter-in-law went to Sunday school. I would meet them there for church. I listened on my computer to Alistair Begg preaching on the providence of God. I left for church and just up the street I noticed a police car. I had never seen a police car on the street. As I passed, I waved at the policeman who I really couldn't see because of the darkened windows.

I was reflecting on the message of the providence of God. I got about three miles from home and got hit. The impact swung me around the intersection, and I grazed another car. The airbags went off and the dust looked like smoke to me. I thought, "I have to get out of this car." I opened the door, but the car was still moving. It finally stopped when it bumped into a curb. I got out and a young man was there. He asked if I needed to sit down or how he could help. I answered that it would help if he would text and call my son.

Soon the police arrived and one of them asked for my license. He looked at it and said, "Dogwood Drive. I was just on a call there." I said, "I waved at you." He smiled and said, "Yes, you did."

God's providence. "And Thy right hand will save me. The Lord will accomplish what concerns me." (Psalm 138). He kept me alive, without breaking any bones. I was badly bruised by the airbags and seat belt. My new knees were safe with only a small bruise on the right knee, which had bumped the middle console.

The next week, my son suggested I start looking for a car. During my research, I checked Craigslist and saw a 2008 Honda Accord, one owner. I learned that it was put up for sale only four minutes before I emailed about it. The owner brought it over and we checked it out. The owner held it for me for two weeks while I got the money together.

To my surprise, two of my sons sent a note with a check from each for $3,000. The insurance company paid full replacement value on my totaled car. My other son paid $600 for the sales tax. I got a wonderful "new to me" car and never paid one dollar. I guess God did not scratch my prayer request off His list.

In February, I learned about an [un]Apologetics Conference being held at a church in Dallas. It was sponsored by the Texas Baptists' Evangelism Department and hosted at my friend Margaret's church. I thought, maybe I could learn how to share Jesus with people in this new culture. The conference main speakers were Mark Mittelberg, a best-selling author and speaker, who focuses in the areas of Christian apologetics and evangelism—Mark's passion is to equip people to share and defend their faith—and Lee Strobel, atheist-turned-Christian, the former award-winning legal editor of *The Chicago Tribune*, and *New York Times* best-selling author of more than twenty books. Lee had just moved to Houston to serve as Professor of Christian Thought at Houston Baptist University.

I received lots of biblical information on how to defend my faith at the Friday night session, but I still wanted more training on how to share my faith. I wrote out my question before the Saturday morning session. "Where can I get training on how to talk with the lost who are entrenched in secularism and have various worldviews?" I prayed that I would get a one-on-one the next morning so I could ask my question.

I was able to talk with the moderator, who was the Texas Baptists' Director of Evangelism. He was involved with 5,400 churches in Texas. He could not point me to such training but said they were going to write one. He suggested I attend one of the outreach training courses on sharing our faith, but it did not address the new culture differences.

Then, I was able to talk with Lee Strobel one-on-one, and he told me about a course. The course explored the theology and practice of personal evangelism, helping students master how to naturally and effectively talk about Jesus in an increasingly diverse and skeptical world. The class was being held at Houston Baptist University on Thursday and Friday evenings and on Saturday that coming weekend.

I went to Houston Baptist University to take the course titled Evangelism: An Unexpected Adventure taught by Lee Strobel and Garry Poole. These veteran leaders in evangelism were heading up the Center for American Evangelism at the university. I was the only gray head among the twenty-year-old students.

That's me—the gray-haired lady second row right.

I had just done something that I had not even dreamed about. I went through a total of seventeen hours of training within nine days on apologetics and non-traditional evangelism. And it answered my question: How do I share Jesus in this upside-down world?

I learned the difference between traditional and non-traditional evangelism and about spiritual discovery groups for non-Christians. I had been praying that the Lord would redefine my life and purpose after David. A fire was ignited in my heart to share Jesus in this new culture. I began asking the Lord how He wanted to use me to reach the unsaved. I wanted to encourage Christians to reach out to their non-Christian friends, neighbors, children, and grandchildren who are a part of this new culture and don't want to come to their church.

It had been eleven months since David went to be with the Lord. Only God knows how He wants me to live out my life without David. Isaiah 54:5 says, "Your husband is your Maker." He directs one step at a time. Just in case, I renewed my passport.

I had two new knees and a better car. I decided to drive to Florida in early March. I wanted to give my son and daughter-in-law a break from me for a while. They had been wonderful supporting me through David's illness, his passing, my knee replacements, the car accident, moments of grief and adjustment. I also needed to take a few months to learn to live alone and not depend on them.

Before I left Texas, my son suggested that I pack everything because they wanted to move to Knoxville. My daughter-in-law's parents lived there, and they hoped to sell the house in Texas and might move while I was in Florida. My daughter-in-law wrote on Facebook that "I think we've been called to care for those that have given their lives to full-time ministry. My parents and my mother-in-law have done just that. Our goal is to build a home to include Dava and build a separate house for my parents. We are excited to see what God will do. He is unfolding a story and I plan to share it as it happens. We are dreaming BIG and right now it seems impossible, but God never ceases to amaze me." So, I packed.

The next month, I drove to Florida to stay in one of my other son's condo for a few months. He had been so thoughtful and generous over the years. Again, I sensed the Lord working through those closest to me. Why should I worry about the future when the Lord said,

> "Look at the birds of the air; they do not sow or reap or store away in barns, and yet your Heavenly Father feeds them. Are you not much more valuable than they? Who of you by worrying can add a single hour to his life?" (Matthew 6:26–27)

My mind flashed back to many years ago when I had completed an internship in Christ-centered counseling. Back to a young lady named Carol. The feeling was sad. Not sad for Carol because she had gone to be with Jesus. I had been sad because of the loss or temporary loss of a friend. Carol and I had shared a lot. Mostly me listening as she told of rejection after rejection in her life. Although Carol would have been twenty-nine, she had gone through more problems, trauma, and hurts than most her age. Carol was my first counselee. Everyone had given up on her and a pastor suggested Carol and I meet. "She needs hope." he said. Carol could not communicate with God; she felt too guilty and unworthy.

We started meeting, and after a few weeks, Carol surrendered her rights to God and gave Him control of her life. Christ became Lord of her life even though she had known Him as her Savior for years. She had a new peace and now talked with her Heavenly Father. She knew she was accepted. She knew her identity in Christ. Then the call came. Carol was dead. She died during the night from natural causes. Carol had graduated and gone to be with Jesus. Judy, her seven-year-old daughter, was now without mother and father. Her father was off somewhere unknown since the divorce.

That morning, as I sat at the breakfast table, something hit the sliding glass door. A sparrow. He fell to the patio floor and breathing his last, he died. Oh God, what a visual message of Your great love for all of us. Yes, God, You do care. We are more valuable than a sparrow to You. You care about Judy. You care about me. You care about everyone.

> "Are not two sparrows sold for a penny? And not one of them will fall to the ground apart from your Father. But even the hairs of your head are all numbered. Fear not, therefore; you are

of more value than many sparrows." (Matthew 10:29–31)

I arrived in the Naples area on March 12. My birthday was a few days away and I really was not looking forward to my first birthday without David. He always made it special. I wanted God to get me through my first birthday without David. I attended Covenant Naples on March 15th and noticed an announcement about a dinner cruise. I stuck it in my Bible and, on Tuesday, I was rereading the announcements and noticed one of the dates for the dinner cruise was on my birthday. I thought, "Is that what you want me to do on my birthday, Lord?" I called Covenant Naples and learned what I suspected, the cruise was full. I asked the lady if she would take my name and number in case God had called ahead. She didn't understand me, so I repeated it, and she laughed and said she would. She called back in five minutes and said they checked the list and discovered one couple on the list was not going to attend. She added my name. God threw me a big birthday party at Bonita Bay's Backwater Jacks with a sunset cruise. Just the kind of thing David would have done.

I started becoming involved at Covenant Naples. Everything I heard preached was right down the line of what I had just learned. Every service added fuel to the fire burning in my heart. I began to ask the Lord to open the door for me to share the non-traditional evangelism techniques I had learned with the pastor.

I joined Covenant Naples where I used to attend when we were in Naples. The congregation is a mission-minded church that gives $2 million through faith promise. Their church budget is less than they give to missions. I wondered what the church was doing regarding a prayer ministry and evangelism. I began praying that they would be a praying church with a passion for evangelism.

A Praying Life had continued to be a passion and I had the director's blessing to hold seminars. I had done *A Praying Life* meetup group and was planning my second one soon. I had written a participant and leader's training manual on non-traditional evangelism and spiritual discovery groups.

On April 19, Pastor Bob sat down next to me while waiting for the Sunday evening service to begin. We had a sixty-second conversation. I continued to pray. On May 7, as I walked toward the church parking lot, Pastor Bob was walking behind me. We had another sixty-second conversation, but this time he said, "Call Cindy and get on my calendar."

I met with Pastor Bob and, then, again with Pastor Bob and Pastor Trent. I asked them to tell me about the church's prayer ministry and what was happening regarding evangelism. They admitted that both were lacking. On July 18th, Pastor Trent and I taught the first non-traditional evangelism training at Covenant Naples. During the next months, I helped start a prayer ministry at the church. Today, Covenant Naples has a wonderful prayer and outreach ministry, thanks to all those who had a passion for prayer and for reaching people. Terry Manley was one of them. She has written two books on prayer, *Prayer Made Simple* and *The Fire on the Inside Changes Everything*.

Yes, God answers prayer. And our spiritual gifts do not age. There is indeed "Life after David" and God has a plan for my life and your life until we take our last breath and go to be with Him.

During one of the first weeks at Covenant Naples, I was sitting in an evening service when John Heerema was introduced and shared information about his international ministry, Biglife. I had not seen John in fourteen years. The man speaking had facial hair, and I was straining to see if it was indeed the John I knew. Yes, it was that same man that I had given a book to read and encouraged to get involved in missions. After the service ended, I went forward to speak to him. He recognized me and gave me a big hug. Then he introduced me to Bill and Marilyn, who later would play a big part in my life.

I had not realized that the book I gave John had had such an impact on his life and future. He gave me a copy of *A Big Life*[6] and, reading it, I learned more about Biglife's impact around the world. He wrote about a night over fourteen years before when I caught him in the parking lot and asked him to become involved in the church's newly formed Missions Committee. He didn't like that at all and wanted to get away from me as fast as he could. But I persisted and, holding a copy of Bob Sjogren's book *Unveiled at Last*, I said, "Well, maybe I could get you to read this. You might find it helpful. Something to pray about." He took the book and, as he drove away, he threw it in the back seat. About two weeks later, he remembered the book and thought he better look at it before he encountered me again. He thought, "I would look foolish if Ms. Missions approached me again, and I hadn't even looked at it."

"As he read on, he found himself increasingly convicted. He came to a sentence that really shook him. He read it over and over. *Are you leading a little life in your own little world?*" He thought. Yes, he was. John surrendered that evening, and the Lord has used him mightily all over the world.

Biglife is a ministry to make disciples who make disciples. It is not a mission-sending organization but one that wins locals to Jesus and they win others. It is not a lengthy process of putting an American in a foreign country where they need to learn the language and culture but one that utilizes local believers who already are well-equipped. John had been a baseball player and used that talent to go into the Middle East with two friends to hold a baseball clinic. You might remember that when I was in Cyprus, I worked on strategy for Narnia (the code name for a

---

6. Peter Hone, *A Big Life: Ordinary People Led by an Extraordinary God* (Tate Publishing Company, Mustang, OK, 2011).

Middle Eastern country.) Here's a note I wrote in my Bible over twenty years ago:

The Lord uses our gifts, skills, and talents to bring glory to Himself. Will you surrender all to Jesus? The very heart of missions is the Christ-centered life. If a Christian does not know who they are in Christ and are living self-centered lives, they cannot be expected to be effectively active in missions. Without total surrender to Jesus, a Christian can only work up some of their leftover or spare time and share their own "gloom" with the unsaved. Give up and let Jesus live His life through you. Give up your "little life" and begin living the "Big Life."

While I was experiencing my "Life after David," my son and daughter-in-law had sold the house in Texas. Their desire was fulfilled. They moved to Knoxville, Tennessee, close to her parents. They rented a townhouse so that they could have time to decide if they were going to build or buy. They wanted to make sure their next home would meet their plans to take care of me and her parents.

I was driving a car with Texas plates and still had a Texas driver's license. My son suggested I come to Knoxville for about three weeks, so they could show me the area and I could begin getting established as a Tennessee resident. Someone at Covenant Naples told me about a good church in Knoxville, Cedar Springs Presbyterian Church. While looking at their website, I noticed they had an extensive prayer ministry. They offered *Starting Point*, a conversation about faith, for those curious about God, Jesus, the Bible, or Christianity—for those who had just begun a relationship with Jesus Christ and those who had some church experience but had been away for a while. I mentioned what I had learned about Cedar Springs and Pastor Trent suggested I check out those ministries while in Knoxville.

Three weeks later, I returned to Florida and before I knew it, the holidays were upon me. Holiday season was especially lonely for me as a new widow. It brought back memories of good times with David and my family. The Lord understands my grief and sorrow. He had a surprise for me.

I had met Michelle and Dan when we both joined the church on the same Sunday. We had kept in touch and they invited me for Thanksgiving dinner. I felt blessed to be included among their family. A luscious meal was followed by games after dinner. At the end of this special day for me, when I was saying goodbye to them, they presented me with a dozen red roses. They had heard that the day after Thanksgiving was my wedding anniversary. I was overwhelmed with their love and God's love through them. Ever since then, they have sent me flowers at that holiday.

Christmas Eve I was alone, and the Lord seemed to say, "It is My birthday! Did you ever consider that I might want to spend the eve of My birthday with you alone?" That got rid of my self-pity fast and sent me into a praise session. I remembered what my friend Samuel Chiang told me, "You are alone and walking the faith journey, may you be blessed to finish the walk well." I pray that I will continue to run the race and finish well. There will be trials and hardships, but all are part of following Christ. Just begin singing this song published in 1845. Your thoughts will begin to be set on things above.

> Give me Jesus
> Give me Jesus
> And you may have all the world
>
> Give me Jesus
> Give me Jesus

CHAPTER TEN

Knoxville and Back

The New Year soon brought news from my Knoxville family that a house had been located that was perfect for all of us. The purchase came the same day that my son lost his job with a major corporation. He sat down with his wife and calculated that they could afford the mortgage payment with just her income. They told me that it would be best if I stayed in Florida until they closed on the house, moved in, and got settled. Mid-April would be a good time for me to come to Knoxville. All the things I had packed up in Texas were awaiting my unpacking in Tennessee. They sent me a video of the area of the house where I would live.

In mid-April, I packed my car and headed to the home where I thought I would live for the rest of my life. I arrived in Knoxville and loved my suite! I had been given the master's suite on the first floor with a deck off from it. I woke up the first morning and lifted my head to look out the window. I gazed off in the distance at a beautiful sunrise over the Smokies. The birds were singing. Flowers blooming. When I looked from my private deck, I was surrounded by tall hardwood trees with some dogwoods mixed in.

The next day, Saturday, was catching up on hugs from my son and daughter-in-law. Her parents came over to welcome me. Saturday night, I said I probably would not go to church with them because I was exhausted from the two-day drive.

Sunday morning, I woke refreshed and thought about church. I looked at the website of Fellowship Church where my son and daughter-in-law were visiting. It was her parent's church. You know that would be the easy way to go, they would drive, park, show me around. I didn't know anyone in Knoxville, and they would introduce me to their friends. But then I looked at the Cedar Springs Presbyterian Church website. I checked out the Sunday school classes and one struck me with this description: "We are a close community of believers sharing our lives and our walk of faith, with a high degree of involvement in missions and in ministry activities within the church and the local community." That sounded like people I wanted to meet. It was only eleven minutes away and I got there early. I found the room and realized it was where He wanted me. The couple leading the class greeted me. I learned they worked with the Refugee Ministry. They told me that Almaz, who coordinates the Refugee Ministry, had been a refugee herself back in 2001. The class started and prayer requests were offered. One prayer request came from the back of the room for an Iranian couple, and it became apparent that it was Almaz speaking. I turned around to get a look at her and planned to talk with her after the class.

After class, I was greeted by several people and, by the time I was free, Almaz had left. I started toward the worship center and there she was. We talked and set up an appointment for Monday to get together. After church, I went to Walmart to do my first grocery shopping and I observed many internationals. I had always been drawn to people from other countries. Walking down one aisle I ran into Almaz. Providential!

Monday, we had agreed to meet in the church café area. When she walked in, she had four Muslim women with her. She introduced me. I walked with them to a knitting class where two church members were there to teach knitting and build relationships. When I walked out with Almaz for our meeting, I was just so overwhelmed with the way God was working here in Knoxville.

We sat in the café area and talked for two hours. Alison, from the Missions Office, came by and I was introduced to her. I had hoped to meet her one day. Then, a man named Mike came into the reception area and Almaz pointed him out and asked if I wanted to meet him. He happened to drop in to return some glasses he had found. He was an Associate Professor of Music at the University of Tennessee (UT) and the coordinator for the church's Chinese summer camp. In the past, I had been involved with many students from Mainland China. We talked about him coming over for dinner soon to meet my son, daughter-in-law, and my granddaughter, Rachel. Rachel was returning in a couple of weeks from a year overseas working with Syrian refugees. He said, if she wanted to be involved in Arabic outreach, he could link her up at UT. Amazing, Lord, my cup overflows. God seemed to have me on a fast track to meet people with common interests.

Tuesday, I got serious about unpacking my boxes. My prayer for the past few days had been for an armoire since we were turning my closet into a morning kitchen. Yesterday afternoon, I drove around looking for one to no avail and learned they were quite expensive. My daughter-in-law forwarded me an ad about one she saw on Craigslist. I learned it was still available and, through texting with the seller, I learned that it was again "providential." The owner texted me, "I noticed your name on the email. This is an odd question, but is your husband's name David and does he have four kids?" I told her yes. She said, "I know some of your family. LOL." She didn't know David had gone to be with the Lord. It turned out that David was her uncle by his first marriage. I was going to meet her the next afternoon. I stood in awe at how the Lord was revealing Himself in those first days in Knoxville.

I had been busy trying to get settled, buying an armoire, and finding someone to deliver it. My son suggested that I get my own separate air conditioner installed. I thought that was a good idea. I was establishing with a primary doctor, getting over my culture shock, and learning the language. I checked out at Walmart the other day and the cashier said, "Do you want a p—?" I asked her to repeat it twice and then I started to guess what she was saying. Finally, I said "pretzel" and she "yes" they were giving them away that day. The accent in Tennessee was foreign to me compared with people in Florida.

Before I left Florida, I had contacted Kathy, Director of Home Missions at Cedar Springs Presbyterian Church. When I walked up to the church area to meet her, out walked a Muslim lady pushing a stroller. Kathy was waiting for me in the café area. We began talking, and along came Almaz. Kathy asked her to meet with us. I asked questions and listened to an overview of Home Missions. I asked Kathy what her biggest need was. As I suspected, she related that she can get people to do things like give food or serve in a food line, arrange clothing at a thrift store, or similar short-term, noncommittal tasks, but she couldn't get church members involved in the long-term mentoring of refugees. I asked, "Why do you suppose that is?" She said, "Because it gets messy. Most Christians are afraid to get involved, don't know how to do it, have limited time because they are so busy at church doing church stuff, fellowshipping, and studying about the Great Commission." She apologized because it is a great church and there is a lot going on but she was being very truthful. She agreed that about 5% were involved in missions/evangelism. This is just what I learned when I studied Evangelism: An Unexpected Adventure with Lee Strobel at Houston Baptist University. I told Kathy my "Life after David" story and how the Lord opened an opportunity to write and teach non-traditional evangelism at Covenant Naples.

Kathy and Almaz said they had been praying recently about how to train Christians to get involved with the multitude of internationals in Knoxville. Kathy suggested I should meet Susan, Director of Women's Ministry, whose burden is how to get people involved with non-Christians. Then, Kathy said she would like me to start by presenting the training to the Missions Staff. As we were concluding our meeting, a large group of internationals, including several Muslim women, came by. They had just finished an English as a Second Language class. I was able to interact with them. After they left, Almaz and I talked about ways the church could get people involved with refugees and immigrants.

A man named Rafeed stopped to talk with Almaz. He was from Iraq, was a psychologist there, and was working in Kroger now. He was excited because soon INVEST was going to start up. It is training and mentoring for professional internationals. We talked about how Almaz had been a refugee from Ethiopia. She worked in the government and was in the parliament, but the only job she could find in America was working at a minimum-paying job.

Almaz invited me to meet with her and the new director of INVEST later that day. She was on the board of the newly formed nonprofit ministry and Cedar Springs Presbyterian Church was partnering with them. Knoxville was one of the government-designated cities for placing refugees when they entered the United States. There were several agencies to help refugees adjust to life in Knoxville. Cedar Springs' refugee ministry was high on their list of ministries.

I learned that 48% of immigrants who came to the United States between 2014 and 2019 held bachelor's degrees or higher. Most could only find entry-level jobs even though they had degrees and experience in many professional areas. I began volunteering with INVEST.

I was feeling comfortable being in Knoxville. It had been a year since I left Texas and, now, I was back among family. It was two years since David went to be with the Lord. Grieving for someone you loved deeply takes time. He was in my thoughts daily.

I was looking forward to my granddaughter coming home soon. Her home had been in Texas when she left for her mission assignment. She had been in the Middle East working among Syrian refugees. I had been her US gatekeeper while she was overseas. A *gatekeeper* is someone who can help coordinate a prayer team and send out prayer requests while on mission. I loved doing this for her since I had had many gatekeepers over the years helping me. We even set up an encrypted email so requests could be sent safely to and from a closed (to the Gospel) country. She had come to Florida and met with my church's mission committee and they decided to support her financially while she was overseas. Rachel and I had lots in common including a love for the peoples of the world.

> "Be sober-minded; be watchful. Your adversary the devil prowls around like a roaring lion, seeking someone to devour." (1 Peter 5:8)

I passed through one of the darkest times in my life. Things happened that made me feel I was in a different world. Relationships were damaged. I will not write the details. Some of you reading this will fill in the blanks probably based on your own experiences. It was a gut-wrenching, emotionally painful time. I was numb and in shock!!

In 1 Peter 5:8, it says to be sober-minded and watchful. A *sober mind* is defined as a controlled, disciplined, and sound mind. Sometimes, the words and actions of others can cause runaway thoughts, fueled by our insecurities and fanned by our adversary.

I started thinking about going to a counselor. I felt I needed someone to talk this through with. I did not have the faintest idea what to do and where I would go. I didn't have any friends in the Knoxville area. I wasn't sure I had the physical strength to move back to Florida. I had a very limited income that I didn't think would support me living on my own. A dear friend from Naples, Kathie, reached out to me. She told me to come stay with her until I figured out what to do. A week later, I packed up and headed back to Florida.

Should we be surprised when we face trials? James 1:2 reads, "Count it all joy, my brothers, when you meet trials of various kinds . . ." That is hard. Maybe impossible as human beings. Maybe brothers can do it, but what about sisters? I just wanted relief from the pain. If only David was alive, he would take care of me. I missed him so much. Grief upon grief. Just a hug from him would make me feel safe and secure. I needed God to intervene. I needed hugs from Him. At the same time, the divine Counselor within me kept saying to keep on, keep on, keeping on.

God was not surprised. In Genesis, we read about Joseph and how his brothers plotted to kill him. One pleaded with his brothers that they should not kill him, so they put him in a pit and eventually sold him for twenty shekels of silver as a slave to some Ishmaelites who took him to Egypt. But twenty years later, Joseph would tell them, "It was not you who sent me here, but God . . ." It is written in Psalm 41:9, "Even my close friend in whom I trusted, who ate my bread, has lifted his heel against me." And, of course, our main example is Jesus. One of His twelve sold him for thirty pieces of silver. "The Lord is my light and my salvation; whom shall I fear? The Lord is the stronghold of my life; of whom shall I be afraid?" (Psalm 27:1)

I read a devotional by Anne Graham Lotz, "Is your focus on your immediate need blinding you to a greater purpose that God is working out? Would you choose to be patient and simply trust Him? Sometimes God does not answer our immediate prayer because He has something greater in store for us."

I heard Jill Briscoe on a radio broadcast say, "A wise person searches for the divine purpose for everything in our brief time on earth. It is a wise man who says, 'Is there a purpose for my being here? Is there something God wants from me? Is there something He wants me to do? Are my days to be filled with purpose and meaning?'" Then, she paraphrased Psalm 139:16. Every day ordained for me is written in His book before one of them comes to be. "I ask every day, Lord. Even _____?" We probably can all fill in that blank with something tough that came into our lives.

Jill went on to say, "And I believe it with all my heart. Nothing can happen to the child of God outside the will of God. . . . Moses was never safer than when he was in the little basket among the crocodiles on the Nile."

I took a couple of days driving back to Florida and was exhausted by the time I reached Kathie's. The next morning, I went out to my car and saw my right back tire was flat. I cried out, "Abba, Father." You know David always handled these things. What should I do? I was so thankful as I thought about the last two days driving seventy miles an hour on I-75. He protected me! I stopped at the condo's gate and asked the guard where the nearest gas station was. He told me just down the road. He said, if I drove slowly, I probably could get there. I pulled up to the air pump and it was coin-operated. Just about that time, a lady came out to empty some trash. She told me it only took quarters and took my dollar and brought back quarters. I got the stem off and started putting air in and midway through a young man came and offered to finish. I was able to drive to Walmart where I got four new tires. I now was driving a car with Tennessee plates and had a Tennessee registration. That would have to be changed to Florida again. I would take care of that soon.

I ended back in my other son's condo. It was a temporary solution since he had promised other relatives and friends that they could use it. It meant moving out when someone was coming and finding temporary housing. He said that I would need to eventually find a permanent place. He suggested I start researching low-income housing and benefits that might be available like food stamps, etc.

As I grieved for David and was heartbroken over what had just happened, I remembered the book I had been writing for several years. I had not touched it in six months, so I pulled out the manuscript. It encouraged me. I had been writing about all the things I saw the Lord doing in my life. I continued to write *Up the River on a Leaky Junk* and finished it within two months. It was published in late 2017.

I was encouraged as I read the Scriptures. "For your Maker is your husband, the Lord of hosts is His name; and the Holy One of Israel is your Redeemer, the God of the whole earth He is called." (Isaiah 54:5) In Psalms, I read, "He upholds the widow and the fatherless" and "He heals the brokenhearted and binds up their wounds."

God's word calls us to "be kind to one another, tenderhearted, forgiving one another, as God in Christ forgave you." (Ephesians 4:32) *Forgiveness* is not a feeling but a decision. It is the choice to pardon, to refuse to punish. When a governor pardons a criminal, he does not excuse the crime or pretend it did not happen. He chooses not to inflict the punishment the criminal deserves. It is the same with us. Forgiveness does not excuse someone's behavior. Forgiveness prevents their behavior from destroying your heart.

Corrie ten Boom, the Holocaust survivor who lost her entire family to the Nazis, likened forgiveness to letting go of a bell rope. When you're pulling on a rope that rings a bell and you let it go, the bell keeps ringing for a while. But if you keep your hands off the rope, the bell will begin to slow and, eventually, it will stop. Forgiveness is letting go of the rope. Tony Evans put it this way, "To refuse to forgive is to burn a bridge over which you yourself must cross, if not now one day." I had to forgive. Whether we were ever reconciled, I had to forgive. I did.

In the meantime, I got back to Covenant Naples and ended up on a team that was putting together a plan for affordable housing. How apropos! I needed affordable housing. I was personally motivated and checked out every source of affordable housing in Collier and Lee Counties. I found that the waiting lists were closed. Most of the waiting lists had a seven-year backlog. With my limited income, I did qualify for the low-income limits. When David died, I lost $15,000 a year in Social Security income. But I would not qualify for renting a regular apartment because I did not make two-and-a-half times the rent. I would probably qualify at the Farm Workers Village in Immokalee (a farm migrant community), but they also had a waiting list. If I went to the women's shelter, which I couldn't do because I did not meet the abuse guidelines, I would have too much income to get an apartment coming from the shelter. I fell below the minimum poverty guidelines. One apartment manager told me because I was below the minimum, I could not rent an apartment unless I found a second person whose income did not exceed the top limit, thus, meeting the income for two people sharing the apartment.

I found a Goodwill apartment for seniors in North Fort Myers. It had a long waiting list. I put my application in. I heard someone mention the Presbyterian Apartments in Fort Myers. I went over there and filled out an application. They said it would be a two-to-three-year wait time. What do I do in the meantime? Being homeless at seventy-seven was a pretty frightening thought.

I was in a quandary. Do I get a job? Then, I will not qualify for low-income housing. And I would have to have a very high paying job in order to qualify to rent a regular apartment. I doubt if I could get such a job at this age. What should I do, Lord?

I continued to pray. I joined a small group at Covenant Naples led by Bill and Marilyn. They were the couple who were with John Heerema the night I saw him at Covenant Naples. They were encouragers and prayer warriors. As we got to know each other, we found we had another mutual friend, Dan O'Berski.

The year had been filled with heartbreak. I was facing homelessness for the first time in my life. At church on Sunday, we were instructed to write out a prayer request and drop it in a box at the altar. I wrote on mine asking the Lord to provide me a place to live. The sermon that morning was on "Seek ye first the kingdom of God and His righteousness and all these things will be added on to you." I bowed my head and told the Lord that I was "all in." No matter what happened, I wanted to tell others about Him. The Lord seemed to remind me that, when we focus on our need, we look at the darkness of the shadow. But when we turn and look full in His wonderful face His light shines on us and the shadow is behind us. Thank you, Lord, for your faithfulness throughout all generations.

> "I will sing of the steadfast love of the Lord, forever; with my mouth I will make known Your faithfulness to all generations." (Psalm 89:1)

> "Your faithfulness endures to all generations; You have established the earth, and it stands fast." (Psalm 119:90)

> "I believe that I shall look upon the goodness of the Lord in the land of the living! Wait for

the Lord; be strong, and let your heart take courage; wait for the Lord!" (Psalm 27:13–14)

Thank you, Lord, you are in control. You have promised in Psalm 92, verses 14–15, "They still bear fruit in old age; they are ever full of sap and green, to declare that the LORD is upright; He is my rock, and there is no unrighteousness in Him."

CHAPTER ELEVEN

God Takes Up My Cause

"How did it get so late so soon? It's night before it's afternoon. December is here before it's June. My goodness how the time has flown. How did it get so late so soon?"—Dr. Seuss

Time does fly and the older I get the faster time flies. It seems like yesterday that I was reading Dr. Seuss books to my three little boys. Now I find myself in my late seventies facing homelessness.

"So even to old age and gray hairs, O God, do not forsake me, until I proclaim Your might to another generation, Your power to all those to come. Your righteousness, O God, reaches the high heavens. You, who have done great things, O God, who is like You?" (Psalm 71:18–19)

It was early January and I was about to launch an all-out blitz to find a place to live. I started putting in applications to every low-income housing I could find in Collier and Lee Counties. Of course, realizing that they each had waiting lists that were at least two to three years. I even considered moving back to Atlanta if I could find an available low-income apartment.

Anne Graham Lotz wrote in her *Joy of My Heart* devotion "Helpless Without Him":

> "Have you wondered, in agony, why God is doing what He's doing? Why He has delayed answering your prayer? Have you reacted to the delay by trying to help Him out and speed things up? Have you turned to a doctor, a lawyer, a counselor, a friend, pop psychology, a neighbor with a sympathetic ear, or a popular TV talk show? Have you resorted to threats, bargaining, and manipulation until you're totally exhausted? Have you come to the absolute end of your rope? One reason God may be delaying His answer to your prayer and postponing His intervention in your situation is to bring you to the end of your own resources. Sometimes God waits in order to allow us time to exhaust every other avenue of help until we finally realize without any doubt or reservation that we are totally helpless without Him. 'I can do nothing on my own. As I hear, I judge, and my judgment is just, because I seek not my own will but the will of Him who sent me.' (John 5:30)"

Yes, Lord, I have! I am at the end of my own resources. I know that only You can rescue me. You say that You are near to the brokenhearted and save those who are crushed in Spirit.

My friend Bill interceded for me. He called our mutual friend, Dan, and told him that I either needed a job or a place to live. Dan told Bill to have me call and come see him. I had been Dan's personal assistant in 2005 until the real estate market crashed.

We met at Dan's commercial real estate office and caught up on the past ten years since we had seen each other. Dan's mom, Susie, met with us. I had met her years before when she visited from Michigan and I was working for Dan. Susie and her husband had just moved to Florida to work with Dan. Little did I know at that time that Susie would become a vital part of my life as I aged. She is now my health care surrogate. We laugh that she will pull the plug on me at the end.

Dan explained that we are part of His Body and we take care of our own. He said he had a little house for me to live in for the rest of my life at no charge. It needed renovation so it might not be move in-ready for a few months.

Not only did he supply a place for me to live, but I had a purpose. His heart was to give back to the Dunbar community in Fort Myers. Dunbar had the highest crime rate and drug addiction in Southwest Florida. His vision was to help those who had not been able to help themselves. Not with handouts but hands up through training leading toward sustainable jobs and affordable housing. I was excited about being a part of his vision and thinking it might be my tenth mission assignment. I had hope as Jeremiah 31:17 said, "There is hope for your future, declares the Lord, and your children shall come back to their own country."

I must admit, driving around the area of Dunbar was like going to another country. Culture shock and fear crept in. The house was not located in the "hood" but on the fringe of the hood. The news didn't help when I realized last night's crime scene was a street not far from my new home.

The place was totally stripped down to the studs. I had some input into the renovation and shared in some of the cost. I was praising the Lord for the renovation of my new "haven" in Fort Myers. It was going to be cozy and a comfortable place to live. It would soon be finished and ready to move in, but I needed to get some of "my favorite things" from Knoxville. The items probably would fit into a twelve-foot moving truck. I prayed that the Lord would provide someone to drive the truck from Knoxville to Fort Myers. I knew God had a plan for moving my things. I hoped He would make it hassle-free or write it on the wall again.

The deacons at Covenant Naples said they would pay for the move and they put out word for the need of someone to fly to Knoxville and drive a small moving truck back to Fort Myers. Claudio volunteered.

A friend told me about someone she knew who was selling a new stackable washer and dryer for $500. I contacted the lady and we agreed that I would buy it, but it had to be moved by a certain date. Now, how was I going to pick it up and move it? God answered the washer/dryer move in an amazing way. Someone at a friend's church offered to move it. The move was delayed and rescheduled. When that day came, we had a tropical storm. It was rescheduled again. The morning of the move, it was cancelled due to the person moving it being sick. I knew I had to move it that day and I started praying.

I went to Lowe's and found I could rent a truck, but I needed some day labor for the move. I hung around Lowe's inquiring of contractors about someone who would like to make some money. I was cautioned to be careful selecting just any man to help. All my effort was a dead end. I thought about students at a nearby college. I left Lowe's not knowing what I was going to do. I stopped to consult with a couple of women at Dan's company. All seemed to be dead ends. I left and sat in the car trying to decide if I was going to turn right or left on Corkscrew Road. I was still praying, but I had no direction. I looked across to the far lane as a truck passed with writing on the side that read, "Rite Now Movers." God had written it on the wall! I called them and they moved it by noon.

The tropical storm continued for four days and dropped twenty inches of rain in the area. The ground was soaked all around my little haven. I hadn't been up there in a couple of days. I thought I would go the next day to move a few more items in. In the morning, I prayed and asked the Lord to reveal if there was anything that might be a problem at my new place.

My day began as I entered the little house and found that it had been flooded. The water had receded except for some puddles here and there in low-lying areas. The floor was not flat all over. A dip here and a little rise there. I mopped up the remaining water. I just finished and another big rainstorm hit. I looked up and water was pouring in under the metal threshold at the door. It was a considerable amount running down the edge of the wall to the other end of the sitting area. I had a few towels and a sponge mop. I won the battle and prayed for a solution.

I was so glad that I was there, or the water might have ruined the new vinyl plank floors. It did run under the mop boards where I could not make sure it was dry.

The last time I prayed that anything hidden would be revealed I learned I had a brother thinking I was an only child. I had written that story in my book that was soon to be published, *Up the River on a Leaky Junk*.

I called the man doing the renovation and he came by. He saw the residue lines the water had left on the floor and the water marks on the mopboards. He said he would get a dehumidifier and we would need to do a mold test later. I called my friend Dan and he texted back that he would get someone to come by and evaluate for a long-term solution. The lot slopes downward from the street to my little house. The downspout drops water just outside the front door.

Claudio met me at the house the next morning to fly to Knoxville and return with the furniture. He parked his van in the yard and we headed for the Punta Gorda Airport. The sun was shining as we arrived at the airport. Off he went and I headed back. I ran into torrential rain around North Fort Myers. I could hardly see and was depending on my Heavenly Father to get me through. The rain let up before I exited the interstate.

I had called a locksmith to change the locks since every sub-contractor had known where the key was hidden during the renovation. It was a cheap lock and I struggled getting in each time. In fact, one day I could not get it unlocked and my neighbor picked the lock. That did not give me a very secure feeling.

I managed to get in and saw the water. That torrential rain I ran into on the way from the airport had been at my house earlier, and now I had water in the bedroom, coming in next to the washer/dryer, in the closet, and on two sides of the living room. It looked like it was coming in under the walls and extended about twelve to eighteen inches from each wall.

I started making calls to the contractor and my friend Dan and many, many calls to the Lord. I just did not know what to do. About that time, the locksmith called and I told him I was dealing with water in the house and perhaps we should reschedule. I had taken my walker up to the house so I would have a place to sit. I just sat there and continued to talk with the Lord about the dilemma. I finally said, "I just can't mop up all this water." Several days ago, when I was an eyewitness to the water coming in under the door, I had mopped it up and suffered for it. Back surgery in the seventies had left scar tissue and arthritis. My right shoulder had a bone spur and arthritis on the AC joint. These areas do not bother me in normal everyday life, but with the mopping motion it had aggravated these conditions. I told the Lord, "I just can't. I am going to lock up and head back to where I was staying." Like the old Kenny Rogers song, "You got to know when to hold 'em, know when to fold 'em and know when to walk away."

Claudio was due to arrive the next afternoon and I was still looking for someone to help him unload the truck. I thought, maybe I would visit some churches in the area to see if they might recommend someone. I backed out of the driveway and saw two boys kicking a ball around in the street. I stopped and introduced myself and learned they lived at the corner house. Guy was a senior in high school and his brother, Joseph, was in the ninth grade. I asked them if they would like to make some money helping me mop up the water. They said they would help and would help unload the truck. I headed back to the house and they told me they would be there in a few minutes. When I tried to unlock the door, it would not open. I called the locksmith to see if I could get him rescheduled to come back. Sadly, I had to turn the boys away until I could get into the house.

The locksmith came and, about the same time, Greg arrived. Dan had called Greg's construction company to come up with a solution. Greg wanted to see where the breaker box was located in case they installed a sump pump As we walked through the house I noticed that the water had receded and there was none to be seen except for the residue of the dirt it left.

After both these men left, I thought I had had enough for the day and I locked up and headed out. I stopped to tell the boys and got to meet their two sisters. During the coming weeks, the boys helped in the yard. One day, Dan dropped off seventeen shrubs and the boys helped plant them. I felt the boys were indeed answers to prayer. God had a bigger plan when He put me in this little house. More than rescuing me, He had neighbors of mine to rescue. They needed Jesus, the eternal rescuer.

The boys had helped unload the truck and unpack. Everything had been moved in including my clothes except my last-minute things. My plan was to move in and live there within the next two to three days.

As I listened to the news, I learned there was a threat of a hurricane heading my way named Irma. People were evacuating. But where should I go? I put out a prayer request. One of my prayer partners in Highlands, North Carolina, said, "Come to my house, I am up over 4,000 feet." It sounded like a "safe haven," so I joined the Great American Race fleeing Irma.

I took the back roads for two days, avoiding I-75 that was a mess. Many had taken that route, and it became a parking lot with no gas available. I left just a couple of days before I was to live in my newly renovated house in Fort Myers. I arrived in Highlands on Friday and, on Monday, Irma arrived and knocked out the power up in the mountains. I hung out in a supermarket that had Wi-Fi during the day. Walking around the market, I saw a young man who had a basket full of groceries. I smiled and commented that I was going to follow him with all those goodies. He said please come to Hamburg Baptist Church at 4:00 p.m. for their soup kitchen. I took him up on it and enjoyed the chili, the corn bread, and especially the sweet fellowship.

During this time, I learned that a neighbor's tree had come down and hit my little house. No power promised for a few days in Highlands, so I took off to drive to Warner Robins just south of Macon, Georgia. At least, I would be heading in the right direction toward Florida. Upon arriving at the hotel, I got an email with the final proof of my book, *Up the River on a Leaky Junk*. That made the next three days move along as I read it one more time before pushing the button to publish. God has a sense of humor. On the tail end of Irma, my book comes out titled *Up the River on a Leaky Junk*.

I moved further south to Brandon, Florida, so I would only have a two-hour drive into Fort Myers from there. I wanted to be fresh when I faced the tree on my house and assessed the condition of my new home. I was to learn more about Philippians 3:8,

> "Indeed, I count everything as loss because of the surpassing worth of knowing Christ Jesus my Lord. For His sake I have suffered the loss of all things and count them as rubbish, in order that I may gain Christ."

I woke about 3:00 a.m. thinking about the tree on my little house and praying the Lord would direct. The next time I woke was about 7 a.m. and I lay in bed thinking surely a "ten-wheeler" had run over me. I prayed, "If I am going to get up, You, dear Lord, are going to have to give me Your strength." I was a slow starter and it took some time for me to shower and get to the coffee station in the hotel. When I arrived, there was a woman standing by the coffee station. She told me she had been waiting for a long time to get coffee. (I was soon to learn that He had placed her there and delayed her coffee awaiting my arrival.) Her name was Rhonda and we struck up a conversation. I told her that I was on the last leg of this Irma race to check out my house that had a tree land on it. She asked me a couple of questions and dragged me to a table as she explained that she was with the Federal Emergency Management Agency (FEMA). She was going to make a disaster relief application for me. The breakfast area was filled with FEMA employees. God knew I needed help before I arrived in Fort Myers and opened the door to a house full of mold. There are times that you may not even know that you have a need and He has already supplied. Today was just such a day.

Rhonda turned out to be a believer, and as we talked about my plight, she said she felt like doing a "Jesus dance." We both knew it was a divine appointment. I met her supervisor, Steve. He told me he was a believer and felt prayer was a priority. It was like I was being carried by my Heavenly Father. He was hugging me. He had taken up my cause. Rhonda completed the application and she hugged me as we parted. She told me someone would be in touch and make an appointment at my Fort Myer's address to do an assessment.

I continued the journey to Fort Myers and my first stop was at the house. Oh, my, that was a big tree that fell. My friend Dan and his crew had removed branches and leaves. The pile filled half the yard. I could see that he had removed the part that had landed on the roof. Dan and his wife had cleaned the mold and painted again.

I praised the Lord that the tree had not destroyed the whole house. I was reminded if Irma had hit a few days later I would have been living there. Praise the Lord, the glass door was not damaged, and my sixty-year-old colored goblet collection was still displayed in each recessed window. When I went inside, I did not see any damage or leaks from the tree landing on the gutter and roof. The only damage inside occurred upon impact of the tree falling when it knocked the folding doors off the closet onto one piece of furniture and the TV. My sixty-year-old rocking chair was not damaged. Got it when I had my first baby.

I am so thankful that my Heavenly Father knows my need and takes care of it before I even am aware of it. The fumes from the demolding process were very strong. Dan said I should wait a week before living there. Mold testing needed to be done, too. A friend told me I could stay at her house until I could get into my new place.

> "For God alone, O my soul, wait in silence, for my hope is from Him. He only is my rock and my salvation, my fortress; I shall not be shaken. On God rests my salvation and my glory; my mighty rock, my refuge is God. Trust in Him at all times, O people; pour out your heart before Him; God is a refuge for us." (Psalm 62:5–8)

During the next year, I learned more about trusting Him. I had a little haven and, even though it was on the edge of the hood, I felt safe and secure. Even when I learned a couple of blocks away there had been a shooting the night before. I had slept like a baby through it all. Now, I had enough room to have friends over for lunch or dinner. I had an extra bedroom in case someone needed a place to stay. I was content. I remembered back to the day that was the darkest in my life. The end of 1 Peter 5 reads in verses 10-11, "And after you have suffered a little while, the God of all grace, who has called you to His eternal glory in Christ, will Himself restore, confirm, strengthen, and establish you. And to Him be the dominion forever and ever."

Recently moving into the neighborhood, I had met several neighbors. Jake was one I had not met yet. He lived across the street. He seemed to come and go in his red truck at times when I was not outside. He would back in, get out, and quickly disappear into his backyard. I had heard about Jake from my friend Dan. He said that Jake had long hair, a wild-looking beard, and might appear somewhat scary, but he was really a teddy bear.

A young couple moved into the other house on Dan's property. One day, her car would not start, and I noticed that Jake was just pulling in. I suggested she might ask him to jump her car. He obliged, and we all stood in the yard getting to know each other during the process. Jake poured out his heart with sentences full of expletives that burned our ears. We listened for over forty-five minutes as he told us how he was always the bad guy and how wounded he had been over the years. By the way, he was not able to get the car started because as he stated, his jumper cables were probably not very good. During our conversation, he had told a story about a birthday past and mentioned his birthday was December 8th.

Later that day Peter, a man who lived next door to Jake, came over and got the car started. He proceeded to tell us that he saw Jake over here and to be careful because he was a "scumbag." I started to pray for Jake after that. His sixteen-year-old son, John, lived with him. Jake had poured out his heart of anger, unforgiveness, and bitterness. I asked my neighbor to pray for Jake. We had had no conversation with Jake since the day he tried to start her car.

As December 8th approached, I told my neighbor that I wanted to get Jake a birthday card and a cake. I picked up a card and we both signed it. I bought a little cake and wrapped it in colorful paper. Now, how I get it to him? As a widow living alone, I felt a little uncomfortable going over and knocking on his door to present the gift. The Lord supplied! I asked Guy who had helped me unpack to deliver it the night before Jake's birthday. He said Jake was really surprised and wondered how we knew it was his birthday.

A couple of days later, I was talking with Guy when a knock came at the door. It was Jake. He came bearing gifts; a decorative Christmas bag with a bag of candy inside, a beautiful glass dish, and a card for me with a $15 movie gift card for my neighbor. He came in and talked about the negative things that had happened to him that week. He referred to us as "different and good people." I suggested that he start hanging around with more good people.

Jake was very open and told me how his long hair and beard were really a way of protecting himself. I acknowledged that I could see that, but I felt he was a man of integrity. We also talked about how we tend to put the bad experiences and negative thoughts into our memory filing cabinet. He said he had a huge bad memory filing cabinet, probably the size of an ocean container unit. We talked about how a present-day comment or action can trigger a reaction that is really drawn from a past hurt. I told Jake that I was praying for him daily and that I believed he was going to begin having good things come into his life. I had gone to a Christmas ornament exchange the day before and came home with a cute little snowman holding a sign saying, "I believe." I gave it to Jake as a reminder that I believed good things were going to come his way.

Jake and I have had some good conversations about Jesus. I still pray that he will trust Jesus and be healed from the old memories controlling his life. Years later, when another hurricane was threatening Fort Myers, he called me to see if I needed anything. I still think he is a man of integrity.

Life in my little haven was an adventure. One morning, I opened the drawer in the bathroom cabinet and up jumped a mouse. I slammed the drawer shut quickly. I told Susie, Dan's mother, who was the contact person for the property. I offered to open the drawer for Susie, but she wasn't sure she wanted to see the mouse. She had a trap set and the hole under the sink sealed.

There was lots of wildlife around my little haven. My neighbor had a snake loose in the house one time. Raccoons were getting in her attic. Well, no wonder! The man who lived in the house next door was feeding them. At least once a day, I would see the momma raccoon running across the yard with her babies trailing behind. They were heading for the dish of food he put out.

I will always remember that day about a year after moving in. One morning, before I got out of bed, I was praying that the Lord would yoke me up and take me where He wanted. I went to a Bible study at my church, the New Hope Presbyterian Church (EPC). When the study finished, I walked out to the parking lot, got in the car, and checked my phone that had been on mute. There was a call from the Presbyterian Apartments. I had put my name on their waiting list two years before.

They were calling to say they had an apartment available, and it was a fast turnaround. I was still number fifty-one on the waiting list. They had called down fifty people, and no one could do a fast move in. They said I had to come over that very day. I called my friend Dan and he met me there. We looked at the apartment and came back to the lobby. Dan had to step out on the porch to catch a conference call. The manager told me that they had one other person who was there to look at the apartment. I wanted to make sure that God wanted me there. I suggested he show the apartment to that person and if she wanted it, I would know it was not for me. While I was waiting, I sat down across from a lady who lived there and introduced myself. I learned she was a Jesus believer and there were a few other believers in the building. The manager came back and said the lady did not take it. I said I would take it, thanking the Lord for confirming it was for me.

Dan and I decided it looked like a good move for me and it appeared to be God's will. It is a standard efficiency with a river view. It is on the second floor, so if there is a fire alarm, I only would have to walk down one flight. It is a HUD low-income apartment with a very reasonable rent. It has good security and, when I get too old to drive, it has transportation to shopping, medical appointments, etc. Yes, it has a low rent but paying for electricity and parking would exceed my budget. Maybe I could get a part time job. I can report to this day that the Lord has provided everything I need and more abundantly than I could ever ask.

I signed a lease and, within twelve days, I moved in. The boys who had helped me at my little haven helped me again. They moved the smaller items. I got an email from one of my prayer partners saying they would like to pay for the larger items to be moved. What a blessing! God provides and gives us the desires of our heart. It is a quiet, safe place to grow old in. Oh, yes, it also has a delightful river view. I can see ducks in the water, boats passing by, squirrels and birds in the trees, neighbors walking their dogs. Places to sit next to the water or eat at the picnic tables. I have seen dolphins jumping up in the water. Although the building faces slightly north east, I can see the residue of sunsets reflecting off the clouds. It is surrounded by other high rises offering high-priced condos. I am a child of the King!

While I was still moving things in, a lady named Phyllis greeted me in the lobby. She asked if I played cards, especially bridge. I told her I did play most any card game and she asked for my phone number. Since that day, we have played hundreds of hands of the card game Hand and Foot and dominoes down by the river.

I started volunteering at the Boys & Girls Club with my friend Susie. It was located on the same property as another low-income housing development. Our vision was to get the moms who lived there involved in mentoring the children in the area. We thought we would start by mentoring the moms, so we put out a flyer inviting them to lunch. Not a one came. We tried other ways to reach out to them. No results. Sometimes He closes doors.

I also mentored at the Dream Center. Fifth graders came after school from Franklin Park Elementary School. Again, children coming from low-income families. Our goal was to eventually mentor the whole family. It seemed like other times God had put me on His fast track. The first week, a mom named Sandra brought her eleven-year-old daughter to join the program. I began to build a relationship with Sandra. I learned she had just moved to the area from South Carolina. She was able to get a manager's job at Wendy's since she had been a Wendy's manager before she moved to Fort Myers.

One day, I met Darius, with whom she had lived since she was sixteen. They had three children. Since they moved here, they had been living with his mother and her man. Seven in a one-bedroom apartment. Sandra was saving to get into an apartment. Sandra was a hardworking lady. Darius worked at day labor off and on. Sandra told me that he blows the money he makes and does not contribute to the savings for an apartment. She said she had been carrying him for twelve years. I suggested the three of us meet. We did get together outside of a McDonald's. I knew that I could help Darius find a full-time job if he was willing. He said he was, so I guided him in putting his plan on paper. We met again to put together a resume.

I heard about a job fair and he agreed to go. I went to a thrift shop and bought him a couple of shirts to wear for interviews. The day came to meet him at the job fair and he texted he could not go. He took a day labor job instead. His mother had encouraged him not to get a full-time job. He was afraid of making a commitment to a permanent job and the responsibility that went with it. I told him he was shortsighted and couldn't see beyond his nose. He never did get a job in all the time I knew him.

Sandra finally got fed up with all his excuses. She had started attending a church and that church was willing to pay for the apartment deposit. She had saved enough to get into her own apartment with her three kids. She had no furniture. I put out the word and through generous donors, we furnished the apartment including all those items one needs. She was so grateful. This is a story duplicated over and over with people who have made poor decisions in life. I found helping some people can be rewarding, but frustrating at the same time. Sometimes nothing you do works. Some folks are more comfortable in their poverty. Others like Sandra take hold of responsibility and just need a hands-up.

After I moved into the Presbyterian Apartments in mid-October, I was put on a waiting list for a parking place. During my first week or two, I constantly bumped into a lady named Betty. We greeted each other with smiles and pleasant words. Where to park was a challenge for me. Each time I approached the building location, I started asking the Lord where He wanted me to park. Besides the reserved spaces for the residents, there were five handicap spots and five guest spaces. There were a few curbside spaces until they put up no parking signs. Next door was a business where we could park during nonbusiness hours.

Betty suddenly died. Phyllis knew about Sandra's household furnishing needs and had inquired about Betty's furnishings. She learned most had already been picked up by a thrift store.

What does that have to do with parking? One day, I arrived back at my building and every parking spot was taken. I circled twice praying about what to do. My car was loaded with Sandra's stuff awaiting her move in. I drove over to the business lot and pulled into a spot. I was uneasy about leaving the car there since it was still business hours. Besides it was near the street and loaded with the stuff. I sat there asking the Lord what I should do. I decided to give it another round to check out parking and said to the Lord, "I feel like Joshua circling Jericho seven times." Around I went and no places even in the back. I stopped near the dumpsters and told the Lord that I had no idea what to do. Then, I saw a man approaching the dumpster pushing a cart and I spotted two folding chairs. I got out of the car and told him I knew someone who might need those chairs. He asked what else I needed. I told him lamps and a toaster. He had a set of matching lamps on the cart and carried them along with the chairs to my car. As he walked to my car he asked, "Are you Phyllis?" I told him no, but I was the person Phyllis was inquiring for. He turned out to be Betty's brother-in-law. I told him I had been driving around looking for a parking place and he said, "I just need to go up and get another small load and then I will be leaving and you can park in Betty's space tonight." He came back with a toaster and some new towels and I pulled into the reserved space number seventy-seven. I find the Lord loves to surprise me when I pray in desperation. When I cannot see any possible solution and He does. I am ever learning more about Him and His faithfulness. Oswald Chambers put it so well in *My Utmost for His Highest*,[7] "Leave Room For God,"

"As servants of God we must learn to make room for Him—to give God 'elbow room.' . . . The way to make room for Him is to expect Him to come, but not in a certain way . . . He may

---

7. James Reimann, editor, *My Utmost for His Highest: The Golden Book of Oswald Chambers—An Updated Edition in Today's Language* (Oswald Chambers Publications Association, Ltd., 1992).

break in at any minute . . . Keep your life so constantly in touch with God that His surprising power can break through at any point. Live in a constant state of expectancy and leave room for God to come in as He decides." I am still learning. He is still carrying me! He reminds me that without faith I cannot please Him.

God has given us so many promises in His Word. One promise that I feel He has given me personally is in 2 Kings 4:1–7. It is the story about the widow who came to Elisha to ask what to do about her creditor who had come to take her children to be his slaves. Elisha asked her what she had in the house and she replied nothing except "a jar of oil." He told her to go by faith and borrow as many vessels as she could. Then, go inside her house and start pouring oil in them. She filled all the vessels she had borrowed. She used the oil to pay her debts so she and her sons could live. For me, it is His promise that my oil will never run out.

> "Though the fig tree should not blossom,
> nor fruit be on the vines,
> the produce of the olive fail
> and the fields yield no food,
> the flock be cut off from the fold
> and there be no herd in the stalls,
> yet I will rejoice in the Lord;
> I will take joy in the God of my salvation.
> God, the Lord, is my strength;
> He makes my feet like the deer's;
> He makes me tread on my high places."
>
> (Habakkuk 3:17–19)

CHAPTER TWELVE

Through It All

ndraé Crouch noted, "Many of the songs I've written
speak to me as far as telling me the process of how to
get through things. 'Through It All' lets me know you
have a lot of experiences in life and you must learn to trust
Jesus."

>Through it all, through it all
>I've learned to trust in Jesus
>I've learned to trust in God
>Through it all, through it all
>I've learned to depend upon His Word.
>
>I've been to lots of places
>And I've seen a lot of faces
>There've been times I felt so all alone
>But in my lonely hours
>Yes, those precious lonely hours
>Jesus let me know that I was His own.

The love of Jesus; so difficult to grasp. We tend to store more
memories from difficult times than the good times. Then, something happens that triggers that old junk. We default to those
not-so-loving moments instead of remembering the blessings

from the hand of Jesus. We often get involved in self-talk and forget that the real battle is in the heavenlies. I am learning that on confusing days I need to praise Him and wait to see what He has planned. I have this reminder taped above my computer keyboard: *Seek God in the present by remembering His goodness in the past and trusting Him for the future.*

A dear friend came to visit me one Saturday morning. She began our conversation by saying that what she was about to tell me she hoped I would receive it in the spirit it was meant. I said, "Oh, oh!" She said it was not an oh, oh. My old memory pattern reverted immediately back to those times in life when I was told how awful I was, and I should be ashamed of myself. Those moments of rejection that led to years of guilt and shame.

My friend told me about her Bunko group which she had been a part of for years. The group decided that each month when they met together, they would bless someone with a financial gift. They changed their name to "Blessed Beyond Bunko." That month's hostess would get to choose the person to be blessed. My friend had chosen me. She handed me a card signed by all the ladies that said, "There are times when what we need the most is to simply sense our Heavenly Father's loving hug drawing us close. May that special hug be a part of your day today." I felt His hug and the hugs from all the ladies who signed the card. Inside was $200. I was overwhelmed by their blessing. That very day, within a few hours, I was taking one of my sons and my daughter-in-law out for dinner to celebrate his 60th birthday. The dinner would be on the Bunko ladies.

As my very good friend Susie O'Berski wrote in her book *We Are the Much More!!!*, "God's patient, loving kindness had gotten through to me. It was not about me. I could not put my hope in anyone but God to meet my needs. My wants. My expectations. They would fail me. Not because they were bad or wrong but because only God would never fail me. Only God could be my hope."

Remember what Anne Graham Lotz wrote:

> "Is your focus on your immediate need blinding you to a greater purpose that God is working out? Would you choose to be patient and simply trust Him? Sometimes God does not answer our immediate prayer because He has something greater in store for us."

There will be trials and hardships, all part of following Christ. It says in Isaiah 30:20–21,

> "And though the Lord give you the bread of adversity and the water of affliction, yet your Teacher will not hide Himself anymore, but your eyes shall see your Teacher. And your ears shall hear a word behind you, saying, 'This is the way, walk in it,' when you turn to the right or when you turn to the left."

> "Therefore, since we are surrounded by so great a cloud of witnesses, let us also lay aside every weight, and sin which clings so closely, and let us run with endurance the race that is set before us, looking to Jesus, the founder and perfecter of our faith, who for the joy that was set before Him endured the cross, despising the shame, and is seated at the right hand of the throne of God." (Hebrews 12:1–2)

As I reflected on life's race behind me, I asked myself, "What did I learn through it all?"

- To pray more—God likes that.
- More about God's love for me—God likes that.
- My future is totally in God's hand—God likes total dependence.
- More about God's Word and His faithfulness—God likes that.
- More about compassion and reaching out to those in need—God likes that.
- More about forgiving others—God likes that.
- More about forgiving myself—God forgave all my sins. I like that.

**Forgetting what lies behind and press on.
Keep on, keep on, keeping on.**

"For I know the plans I have for you, declares the Lord, plans for welfare and not for evil, to give you a future and a hope." (Jeremiah 29:11)

THE BEST IS YET TO COME!

End Note

You may say, "The title of this book just doesn't make sense." I have prayed about that.

It didn't make sense to me. I asked the Lord for a new title and nothing came. Then, I realized as I looked back on the olive trees that I saw on my four mission assignments around the Mediterranean, those olive trees were silent! As I was going through experiences in life; good, bad and ugly, the olive trees were silent. Isn't it a blessing that olive trees can't talk? If we were able to see and hear what they see and hear, we would be gnarled, too!

"*Gnarled*—knobbly, rough, and twisted, especially with age."

What can we learn from the olive tree? The olive branch has been a symbol of peace to the world, and we often hear the expression "extending an olive branch" to another person as a desire for peace.

Be at peace with one another.

Having witnessed Jesus dying on the cross and resurrecting three days later, they would bow low to the ground in awe of the Savior. The olive trees would point their branches toward heaven and sing hallelujah to the King of Kings.

Do you have peace with God?

How will you respond to Jesus? He stands with open arms inviting you to come.

Come, come, come!

We all know we have sinned. We have all done things that are displeasing to God. The punishment that we have earned for our sins is death. Not just physical death, but eternal death! God's solution to our sin is a gift that can't be earned.

> "For God so loved the world, that He gave His only Son, that whoever believes in Him should not perish but have eternal life." (John 3:16)

Jesus Christ died for us! Jesus' death on the cross paid the price for our sins. Jesus' resurrection proves that God accepted Jesus' death as the payment for our sins and we are given new life.

Because of Jesus' death on our behalf, all we need to do is believe in Him, trusting His death as the payment for our sins, and we will be saved!

> "For everyone who calls on the name of the Lord will be saved." (Romans 10:13)

Jesus died to pay the penalty for our sins and rescue us from eternal death. Salvation, the forgiveness of sins, is available to anyone who will trust in Jesus Christ as their Lord and Savior.

"Therefore, since we have been justified through faith, we have peace with God through our Lord Jesus Christ." (Romans 5:1)

"Therefore, there is now no condemnation for those who are in Christ Jesus." (Romans 8:1)

"For I am sure that neither death nor life, nor angels nor rulers, nor things present nor things to come, nor powers, nor height nor depth, nor anything else in all creation, will be able to separate us from the love of God in Christ Jesus our Lord." (Romans 8:38–39)

Would you like to receive Jesus as your Savior? If so, here is a simple prayer you can pray to God. Saying this prayer is a way to declare to God that you are relying on Jesus Christ for your salvation. The words themselves will not save you. Only faith in Jesus Christ can provide salvation and new life!

"Dear God, I know that I have sinned against You and I am deserving of punishment. But Jesus Christ took the punishment that I deserve so that through faith in Him I could be forgiven. With Your help, I place my trust in You for salvation. Thank You for Your wonderful grace and forgiveness and the gift of eternal life! I ask that You direct my life from now on. Amen!"

THE BEST IS YET TO COME!

Suggested Readings

A Big Life: Ordinary People Led by an Extraordinary God, Peter Hone, Tate Publishing, Mustang, OK, 2011.

A Praying Life: Connecting with God in a Distracting World, Paul E. Miller, NavPress, Colorado Springs, CO, 2009.

Basic Christianity, 50th anniversary edition, John Stott, Inter-Varsity Press, London, 2008.

Handbook to Happiness, Charles R. Solomon, Tyndale House, Denver, CO, 1971, 1989, 1999.

Lifetime Guarantee: Making Your Christian Life Work and What to Do When It Doesn't, Bill Gillham, Harvest House Publishers, Eugene, OR, 1993.

My Utmost for His Highest: The Golden Book of Oswald Chambers—An Updated Edition in Today's Language, edited by James Reimann, Oswald Chambers Publications Association, Ltd., 1992.

Prayerwalking: Praying On-Site with Insight, Steve Hawthorne and Graham Kendrick, Charisma House, Lake Mary, FL, 1993.

The Normal Christian Life, Watchman Nee, Tyndale House Publishers, Inc., Carol Stream, IL, 1977.

Unveiled at Last: Discover God's Hidden Message from Genesis to Revelation, Bob Sjogren, YWAM Publishing, Edmonds, WA, 1996.

www.ingramcontent.com/pod-product-compliance
Lightning Source LLC
LaVergne TN
LVHW021451080426
835509LV00018B/2246